Halloween Favorites in Plastic

Charlene Pinkerton

4880 Lower Valley Road, Atglen, PA 19310

Dedicated to Emily and Adeline Wunsch, who were my Mom and Auntie Ad.

Book Design by Laurie A. Smucker

ISBN: 0-7643-0509-3
Printed in China
1 2 3 4

Published by Schiffer Publishing Ltd.
4880 Lower Valley Road
Atglen, PA 19310
Phone: (610) 593-1777; Fax: (610) 593-2002
E-mail: schifferbk@aol.com
Please write for a free catalog.
This book may be purchased from the publisher.
Please include $3.95 for shipping.
Try your bookstore first.

We are interested in hearing from authors
with book ideas on related subjects.

Contents

Acknowledgments

Mark and Judy Craven of Snohomish, Washington, opened their home to me and helped my husband with the photography of their wonderful collection. Mark sent updated photographs to me whenever he added something new to the collection and kept me up to date on exciting things he found. Dave and Ginny Wellington and Cindy and George Grew encouraged me to complete this book. And I am forever grateful to the following people for their help:

Don Featherstone of Union Products; Joe Danowski of the E. Rosen Co./Rosbro; Ann and Richard Davidson; Eric and Cynthia Herrman; Bob Albachor; Tom Weber; Randy Pinkerton; Joel Berman; Bernadean Strab; Jenny Tarrant; Paul Schofield; John Forester; Christian and Kathleen Eric; Sam Dipoli; Tana DeRenzo; Richard Miller; Keith Lauer of the Plastics Museum; Tom Prichard of Empire Products; Larry Geller; Patty Gallagher Mangus of Blinkys; and Bertram Cohen of Irwin Plastic Corp. I thank my son, Jordan Shock, for his computer help and my husband, Ron Pinkerton, for everything.

Craven Farms tractor with load of fresh pumpkins.

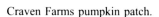

Craven Farms pumpkin patch.

Introduction

Halloween in the Midwest

Growing up in the Midwest during the 1940s and 1950s, and experiencing the different seasons into October and Halloween was an enriching childhood experience. The Midwestern classic *Injun Summer* by John T. McCutcheon was published every year in the Chicago Tribune and heralded the onset of autumn and Halloween. Living in the city, the Farmers Market was where I first saw the pumpkins and Indian corn being brought in from the surrounding farms. To this day the first pumpkin sighting stirs up the memories of that time so vividly that I can still see the papier-mâché and hard plastic jack-o'-lanterns at the old five-and-dime store and the candy containers sitting on the counters at the soda fountains wrapped in cellophane. I can still feel the wooden floors that creaked and felt so good to walk on as I went up and down the aisles in the old stores taking in all the autumn decorations and colors.

My brothers and I would gather our costumes to go trick or treating. Chuck would be a pilot, Dave a policeman, and I was always a ballerina. In Indiana during the 1940s and '50s, there was beggars night before Halloween night. We went out trick or treating on both nights. The leaves would be off the trees by now and the big oaks and maples looked spooky as we tramped over the sidewalks up to the front doors and held out our bags for our treats.

The porches were decorated with jack-o'-lanterns and there were lots of parties to go to at school and Campfire Girls. I always loved the decorations as well as the ghost games we played, the prizes for the best costumes and the treasure hunts. It is from these memories that I went on to write this collectors' guide that will help to answer some of the questions about the Halloween plastics.

Halloween Decorating and History

Halloween is that one exciting night a year when a person experiences fear, fantasy, and mystery at the same time. Decorations have always played a part in this trilogy, and each year they get more elaborate.

The first decorations were vegetables carved out and lit with a candle inside to scare away evil spirits. The holiday comes from Scotland. The first trick or treaters could have been farmers who went house to house soliciting food for the village Halloween festival. Health and prosperity was promised to cheerful givers and threats were often made against tight-fisted donors. It is believed that the Scottish and the Irish people brought the holiday to the United States and Americans began to celebrate Halloween in the last half of the nineteenth century.

The jack-o'-lantern symbolizes the holiday spirit and no matter how many other decorations are used, the pumpkin still gets carved as part of the holiday tradition. Now instead of being used to chase away evil spirits, the jack-o'-lantern lights the porches to welcome the trick or treaters. The jack-o'-lantern is so named because of a legend from Ireland about a man named Jack who wandered the earth carrying a lantern. He was too wicked for heaven and had been thrown out of hell for playing tricks on the devil.

Decorating is a creative outlet for many people. It is a way to share our culture. Americans began to decorate with pieces made in Germany. Postcards from the Victorian or late Art Nouveau era feature precious, rosy cheeked children bobbing for apples. The beginning of the Art Deco era brought us the beautiful flapper-style decorations depicting elves and fairies of European folklore. During the 1930s and 1940s, artists created the beginning of an American style of decorations characterized by the American love of the movies, the artwork in the popular Sunday cartoons and comic books, and an overall design change made to be less frightening to children. In the late 1940s and 1950s, the hard plastic era and the end of the Art Deco period, the decorations were beginning to give glimpses of our plastic future. Soon the majority of our old paper, metal, and bisque decorations would be made of plastic.

The jack-o'-lanterns and small plastic Halloween toy decorations from the 1960s are now gaining popularity. The paper cutouts of the 1960s, 1970s, 1980s, and 1990s have not been as popular as the plastic toys. The 1970s was a low period for holiday decorations even though Hallmark introduced a quality line of plastics at that time. Better quality decorations followed in the 1980s and 1990s, and the new lights are wonderful. Also, the arts-and-crafts movement of the last two decades has given us new and reproduced Halloween pieces to collect.

Victorian era/Art Nouveau postcard.

Early Art Deco crepe paper.

Later Art Deco E. Rosen sucker holder 1940s-1950s.

New modern witch.

The Hard Plastic Era, Made in the U.S.A.

The Golden Age of plastic toys, The Hard Plastic Era, began after World War II. This is the time of the birth of the Ginny doll by Vogue, the Tony doll by Ideal, the Terri Lee doll, and all of the other beautifully designed hard-plastic dolls. The five-and-dime store was flourishing, and no one dreamed that there would be a Kmart in our future. Colorful, hard plastic toys were being supplied by such company's as Renwal, Knickerbocker, Ideal, Plasco, Acme, and Marx—all highly collectible today. These toys were more comfortable to the touch than metal and were supposed to last a lifetime. They didn't last, however, which is why old plastic is valuable today. Halloween plastics from the end of the Art Deco period are the most valuable of all.

People were amazed to see old plastic become so valuable during the 1980s. Collectors saw these items as part of their childhood and bought them for nostalgic reasons. Most of the better pieces in this guide are hard to find now. Old Halloween hard plastic will soon be as hard to find as the older papier-mâché and German candy containers.

There were several makers of hard plastic candy containers and novelty toys: Knickerbocker, Irwin Plastics, E. Rosen/Rosbro Plastics, and Tico Toys Inc. were some of the leading manufactures of these products. Knickerbocker made bunnies and chicks with rattles, pull toys, banks, Easter bunnies dressed in skirts and pants, and other Easter basket toys. Irwin Plastics made lambs and other Easter basket toys with rattles as well as Christmas and Easter candy containers. E. Rosen/Rosbro Plastics made candy containers for all the holidays and filled them with candy. These were some of the last of the hard plastic novelty toys to be made in the United States. After the early 1960s, dime store and novelties toys were being made mostly of vinyl, and mostly outside of the United States. The hard plastic era, made in the U.S.A., ended. There were so many of these toys and candy containers made that this guide shows only a small portion of these collectibles.

A variety of hard plastic era novelty toy and holiday candy containers.

Plastic Is Not New

The word plastic comes from the Greek word *plasticos* meaning "able to be molded." Chinese and other ancient cultures discovered that natural substances such as tortoise shell, horn, and tree sap could being molded into different shapes with heat and pressure. These were the first inventors of plastic, though the person commonly credited with the innovation was an American printer.

A $10,000 reward for a product to replace ivory used in billiard balls incited an American printer by the name if John Hyatt to claim the prize. John's formula for a partially synthetic plastic created from cellulose nitrate derived from tree fibers won him the reward and his place in history as a modern plastic inventor. Although John patented his plastic in 1870, the Germans went on to become the leaders of plastic manufacturing between 1878 and 1900. They used the process to create dolls, trinkets, and small household items that became very popular because they were light and cheap as well as easily made. Hyatt's company began to make dolls around 1880 from scrap material. By 1890 tub toys, rattles, and curio items being sold around the world. Fifty years later plastic was commonplace in the toy and automotive industries.

Even as early as 1942 the DuPont Company advertised that some cars contained as many as 230 parts that were made out of plastic. Around 1937, the Dow Chemical Company introduced a new substance for molding called polystyrene or, as Dow called it, styron. Next came injection molding a process of heating the plastic to very controlled temperatures and injecting it under heavy pressure into hardened steel molds producing great products at fast production rates. This new plastic, along with a new process of injection molding, created excellent products that needed little trimming or touchup, even with the most elaborate designs. This polystyrene cost less and weighed less than the previous cellulose acetate and the polystyrene had a shiner look than the flat, yellowish look of cellulose acetate.

By the end of the 1950s, the beginning of the Barbie® doll era, a new type of plastic started to be used. This soft plastic or polyethylene made the products less likely to break when dropped or hit. By the end of the 1960s, polyethylene had replaced polystyrene. The plastic used by Hallmark and Fun World as well as other companies during the last four decades is not polystyrene but an ever changing compound of plastic varying in quality as it goes from country to country in the manufacturing world.

Inexpensive celluloid owl from the 1930s. Inexpensive, more durable vinyl witch, new 1996. (*Author's collection.*)

Historical study of plastic. Celluloid, hard plastic, more durable hard plastic, inexpensive vinyl. (*Author's collection.*)

Plastics Museum

The National Plastics Center and Museum opened in Leominster, Massachusetts, in 1992. Leominster is the pioneer city of the plastics industry in the United States. The museum is a non-profit institution dedicated to preserving the past, addressing the present, and promoting the future of plastics though public education and awareness. A special exhibit is The Plastic Hall of Fame where you can learn about the pioneers who helped create the plastic industry. There are rare artifacts and first-of-it's-kind machinery used to mass produce plastic products. Exhibits of celluloid and plastic toys are rotated seasonally and there are special areas of the museum where children are taught about the recycling process and are shown how popular toys are made. Programs include a discovery corner where construction and invention are going on and all ages watch as plastic bottles are turned into souvenirs. Interpreters explain the early days of the plastic industry, illustrating their talks with rare and unusual artifacts from some of the most famous plastic collections in the United States.

Hints for Buying and Selling Old Hard Plastic or Polystyrene

1. There should be no breakage. Breakage or loss of parts greatly reduces the value. Early Polystyrene becomes brittle with age.

2. Plastic does not repair well. The collectible should be of good color and not faded. Fading is caused by excessive, prolonged exposure to light.

3. The prices herein are for mint condition pieces, most pieces are not mint.

4. Plastic prices are determined by rarity, age, color, size, fragility, and quality of plastic.

5. Early polystyrene plastic sometimes shows its age with small fractures, like old pottery. This is not a bad flaw as long as part of the piece is not missing or broken off.

6. Toys on wheels command a higher price than the same toy without wheels, 35 to 50 percent more.

7. Keep plastics stored in a cool area, wrapped in clean, white tissue paper or inside an airtight case.

8. Keep early polystyrene from mixing with early vinyl. The two are drawn together and cause damage. Do not wrap the cords around the bases of polystyrene items and do not use rubber bands on these pieces.

9. Light scratches can be buffed out using Happich Simichrome polish.

10. Halloween plastics can be reproduced. Attempted reproductions of polystyrene that have been done in the Eastern countries have a dull finish, are smaller, have rough mold marks, and are easily spotted by a plastic expert. Renwal doll furniture was reproduced in a brown color only. The same mold mark was used with Renwal covered over.

It is hard to reproduce an exact replica of polystyrene because the molding process uses large steel molds that would be very difficult to match with original mold sizes and flash lines. It would also be hard to produce the same artistry and colors.

Hints for Buying and Selling Plastic or Polyethylene

1. Buy as clean a piece as possible. Vinyl toys get dirty easily. Some scrapes are very hard to remove

2. Use Simple Green for dirt and a fiberglass eraser for bad spots.

3. Buy unique pieces.

Recycling as a Hobby

There is an ecological responsibility that we all have to recycle plastic. It makes good sense to keep it for display rather than throwing it away. Collectors are recycling as part of their hobby. By doing this we preserve our cultural heritage. Our ancient mounds will contain some great plastic toys.

"Andy we must always remember to recycle and reuse our plastic Halloween decorations!" (*Author's collection.*)

Chapter One
E. Rosen/Rosbro Plastics, Tico Toys Inc.

The E. Rosen/Rosbro style was to mold jack-o'-lanterns, cats, witches, clowns, donkeys, and other interesting characters into very delicate plastic toys that carried candies wrapped in colorful cellophane. They made thousands of these toys from 1946 through the early 1960s. Their plastic composition changed in the 1960s and '70s to a more durable, rubberized plastic, and production eventually went to Hong Kong.

E. Rosen is the parent company of Schoolhouse Inc. in Pawtucket, Rhode Island. Schoolhouse has been an American distributor of holiday candies since 1911. E. Rosen and Rosbro plastics are the same family company. The older Rosbro items are from Providence, Rhode Island. Some items are embossed "Rosbro," others are not even though some were made into the 1960s. The candy was always tagged "E. Rosen Co." Tico Toys Inc. products were used by E. Rosen before the 1950s. Some of the older, unmarked molds are Tico Toys Inc., Pawtucket, Rhode Island. The Tico Toys molds were eventually purchased by E. Rosen.

Rosbro and Tico Toys used a very shiny plastic and put small toys on wheels similar to the toys at the beginning of the century during the Victorian Era. They molded them into different colors for different holidays and occasions. Collectors like to find these toys for all of the holidays, in different colors and with different paint. The wheels are quite important since they add more value to the price of the toy. The same toys were made without wheels. The older toys are on wheels.

The name embossed on the candy containers is "Rosbro Plastics, Providence, Rhode Island." This mark is sometimes hard to find. The mark on the Trojan Horse is inside the leg. The mark on the clowns is found on the back. An Easter rabbit pushing a wheelbarrow is Rosbro, but the only mark is on the wheelbarrow, so if you find the rabbit alone you must know the Rosbro style to properly identify it. Learn to recognize the Rosbro/Tico Toys style of toys, the molds, paint combinations, type of wheels and the type of plastic used.

Today the E. Rosen Co. is located in Pawtucket, Rhode Island. They are still in the candy container business. Schoolhouse candy has a small retail store in Pawtucket, Rhode Island, open to the public.

Cat pushing jack-o'-lantern on wheels, 1950s, molded by Tico Toys/Rosbro, not marked. 5.25" x 6.75", orange plastic, green and black paint; yellow wheels. (*Courtesy of Mark and Judy Craven.*) $250-275.

White cat pushing jack-o'-lantern on wheels, 1950s, molded by Tico Toys/Rosbro, not marked. 5.25" x 6.75", white plastic, orange and black paint; yellow wheels, rare. (*Courtesy of Ann and Rich Davidson.*) $300-350.

Cat pushing jack-o'-lantern on platform on wheels, 1940s, molded by Tico Toys, not marked, 6.13" x 6.75", orange plastic, green and black paint, green platform, yellow wheels. (*Courtesy of Mark and Judy Craven.*) $300-375.

Cat pushing jack-o'-lantern on platform, no wheels, molded by Tico Toys Inc. $75-125

Cat pushing jack-o'-lantern on wheels, late 1950s, molded by Rosbro, not marked, 5.25" x 6.75", orange plastic, black paint, yellow wheels. Poorer quality than other cats. (*Courtesy of Mark and Judy Craven.*) $125-150.

Group of Rosbro/Tico Toys cats.

Cat pushing jack-o'-lantern on platform #821, molded by Tico Toys/Rosbro, not marked, 5.50" x 6.50", orange plastic, green and black paint, black platform, electrified by Miller Electric Co., Pawtucket, Rhode Island, 1952. (*Courtesy of George and Cindy Grew.*) $300-350.

Advertisment for Halloween novelties from Nicolett Novelty House, 320 Nicolett Avenue, Minneapolis, Minnesota, dated September 18, 1952. (*Courtesy of Mark and Judy Craven.*)

Cat pushing jack-o'-lantern on wheels, early 1950s, molded by Tico Toy/Rosbro, not marked 5.25" x 6.75", orange plastic green and black paint, replaced wheels. *Courtesy of Richard Miller* $75-125. (*photo by Richard Miller*)

Late Art Deco sucker holder. E. Rosen did a lot of different kinds of candy distribution using plastic and paper. $25-45.

Party whistle, pirate with cape on wheels, not marked, early 1950s, molded by Tico Toys/Rosbro, 4.75" x 4", orange plastic, black paint, replaced green wheels. (*Courtesy of Mark and Judy Craven.*) $45-55.

Party whistle, witch with horn on wheels, not marked, early 1950s, molded by Tico Toys/Rosbro, 4.75" x 4", orange plastic, black paint, black wheels, cat painted on skirt. (*Courtesy of Mark and Judy Craven.*) $55-75.

Party whistle, party goer with jack-o'-lantern on back, not marked, early 1950s, molded by Tico Toys/Rosbro, 4.75" x 4", orange plastic, black paint, green wheels. (*Courtesy of Mark and Judy Craven.*) $55-75.

Cowboy with western horse, wheels missing, early 1950s, molded by Tico Toys/Rosbro, not marked, 5" x 4.25", orange plastic, black paint, rare. There is also a cowgirl. (*Courtesy Richard Miller/ Photo by Richard Miller.*) $250-275.

Party whistle, cat with saxophone, early 1950s, molded by Tico Toys/Rosbro, not marked 4.75" x 4", orange plastic, black paint, black and orange wheels. (*Courtesy of Mark and Judy Craven.*) $55-75.

Cowboy on western horse on wheels, early 1950s, molded by Tico Toys/Rosbro, not marked 5" x 4.25", black horse, orange wheels, orange cowboy with black paint, very rare. (*Courtesy of Mark and Judy Craven.*) $275-325.

Cowboy with western horse pulling Valentine wagon, early 1950s molded by Tico Toys/Rosbro, not marked, 5.50" x 8", white plastic, red and black paint, face painted flesh color, red and white wheels, holiday crossover candy container using same figures. (*Courtesy of Mark and Judy Craven.*) $300-375.

Pirate Cat ornament with jack-o'-lantern body and top hat, missing plastic hole for hanging, early 1950s, molded by Tico Toys/ Rosbro, not marked, 3.13" x 2", orange plastic, black, white, and green paint. (*Courtesy of Mark and Judy Craven.*) $25-30.

Cat ornament with jack-o'-lantern body and top hat, plastic hole for hanging is missing, early 1950s, molded by Tico Toys/Rosbro, not marked 3.13" x 2", orange plastic, black and white paint. (*Courtesy of George and Cindy Grew.*) $25-30.

Witch on motorcycle, early 1950s, molded by Tico Toys/Rosbro, not marked, 4.88" x 6.88", orange plastic witch and motorcycle, green wheels, black paint. (*Author's collection.*) $350-400.

Pirate cat ornament with top hat, with hole for hanging. (*Author's collection.*) $45-55.

Group Rosbro/Tico Toys witches. (*Author's collection.*)

Red witch on white motorcycle, early 1950s, molded by Tico Toys/Rosbro, not marked 4.88" x 6.88", red paint, yellow wheels, rare. (*Courtesy of Mark and Judy Craven.*) $400-450.

Black witch on white motorcycle, early 1950s, molded by Tico Toys/Rosbro, not marked 4.88" x 6.88", black paint, orange wheels, rare. (*Courtesy of Ann and Rich Davidson.*) $400-450.

17

Woolworth advertisement for E. Rosen candy containers, early 1950s. Above advertisement for hard plastic jack-o'-lantern. (*Courtesy of George and Cindy Grew.*) $50-75.

Springy flat witch going over full moon, 1950s, molded by Tico Toys/Rosbro, not marked, orange moon, black witch, black cat on green platform. (*Courtesy of Mark and Judy Craven.*) $55-75

Springy flat witch going over half moon, 1950s, molded by Tico Toys/Rosbro, not marked, 6.25" x 3.63", orange moon, yellow witch, black and orange cat on green platform. (*Courtesy Mark and Judy Craven.*) $55-75.

Springy flat witch going over half moon, 1950s, molded by Tico Toys/Rosbro, not marked, 6.25" x 3.63", yellow half moon, black witch, yellow and black cat on green platform. (*Courtesy of Mark and Judy Craven.*) $55-75.

Sringy flat witch going over full moon, 1950s, molded by Tico Toys/ Rosbro, not marked, yellow moon, black and orange witch, black cat on green platform. (*Courtesy of Mark and Judy Craven.*) $55-75.

Black witch riding rocket, 1950s, molded by Tico Toys/Rosbro, not marked, 6" x 3.5", black plastic, orange paint, orange wheels. (*Courtesy of Mark and Judy Craven*) $300-350.

Orange witch riding rocket, replaced wheels, 1950s, molded by Tico Toys/Rosbro not marked, 6" x 3.5", orange plastic, black paint, replaced yellow wheels. (*Courtesy of Mark and Judy Craven.*) $200-250.

Yellow Clowns on wheels and off wheels, 1950s, holiday crossover candy containers for Easter, embossed "Rosbro Plastics, Providence, Rhode Island." Clown on left: 6.50" x 3.50", green platform, yellow wheels. $85-115. Clown on right: 5.5" x 3.13", yellow plastic, blue and red paint, black hat. $65-85. (*Author's collection*)

Zook, a playful prankster clown on wheels, 1950s, embossed "Rosbro Plastics, Providence, Rhode Island, " 6.5" x 3", orange plastic, black paint, white hat, black platform, orange wheels. These clowns were made for all occasions. (*Author's collection.*) $85-115.

Pete the Clown, no wheels, 1950s, embossed, Rosbro Plastics, Providence, Rhode Island, 5.5" x 3.13", orange plastic, black paint with cat on leg, white hat. (*Courtesy of Mark and Judy Craven.*) $65-85.

Pink clown on wheels, 1950s, embossed "Rosbro Plastics, Providence, Rhode Island." Holiday crossover candy containers for Easter, 6.5" x 3.13", pink plastic, red and blue paint, green platform on red wheels. (*Author's collection.*) $85-115.

Cat holding jack-o'-lantern, 1950s, molded by Tico Toys/Rosbro, not marked, 5" x 3.5", orange plastic, black paint. (*Courtesy of Mark and Judy Craven.*) $65-85.

White clown on scooter, white clown on wheels, 1950s, both embossed "Rosbro Plastics Providence, Rhode Island." Holiday crossover candy containers for Christmas, white plastic, red, blue, and yellow paint; yellow wheels. Clown on scooter 5.5" x 6.75", $110-165. Clown on wheels, 6.5" x 3.13", $85-115. (Author's collection.)

Cat on wheels with jack-o'-lantern, 1950s, molded by Tico Toys/Rosbro, not marked, 5.75" x 3.25", orange plastic, black paint, green platform, yellow wheels. (*Courtesy of Richard Miller/Photo by Richard Miller.*) $85-115.

Cat on wheels missing jack-o'-lantern, 1950s, molded by Tico Toys/ Rosbro, not marked, 5.75" x 3.25", orange plastic, green and black paint, green platform, yellow wheels. (*Courtesy of Mark and Judy Craven.*) $85-100.

Black Trojan horse, 1950s, embossed "Rosbro Plastics, Providence, Rhode Island, " 5.5" x 5", black plastic, orange wheels. (*Courtesy of Dave and Ginny Wellington.*) $50-75.

Orange Trojan horse, 1950s, embossed "Rosbro Plastics, Providence, Rhode Island, " 5.5" x 5", orange plastic, black wheels, original candy inside. (*Courtesy of Mark and Judy Craven.*) $50-85.

Cat no jack-o'-lantern, 1950, molded by Tico Toys/Rosbro, not marked, 5" x 3.5", orange plastic, black and green paint. (*Courtesy of Mark and Judy Craven.*) $65-85.

Black cat pumpkin body, 1950s, molded by Tico Toys/Rosbro, not marked, 4.5" x 3.5", orange plastic painted black head, black wheels. (*Courtesy of Mark and Judy Craven.*) $65-85.

Trojan horse crossover holiday candy container for Christmas, early 1950s, embossed "Rosbro Plastics, Providence, Rhode Island, " 5.5" x 5", clear plastic, red paint, green wheels. (*Author's collection.*) $65-85.

Black cat with orange whiskers, 1950s, molded by Tico Toys/ Rosbro, not marked, 3.5" x 3", black plastic orange painted whiskers and eyes. (*Courtesy of Mark and Judy Craven.*) $40-50.

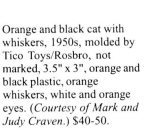

Orange and black cat with whiskers, 1950s, molded by Tico Toys/Rosbro, not marked, 3.5" x 3", orange and black plastic, orange whiskers, white and orange eyes. (*Courtesy of Mark and Judy Craven.*) $40-50.

Orange cat pumpkin body, 1950s, molded by Tico Toys/Rosbro, not marked, 4.5" x 3.5", orange plastic, orange head, black paint, black wheels. (*Courtesy of Dave and Ginny Wellington.*) $65-85.

Orange cat with whiskers, 1950s, molded by Tico Toys/Rosbro, not marked, 3.5" x 3", orange plastic, black and white eyes. (*Courtesy of Mark and Judy Craven.*) $40-50.

Accordian player jack-o'-lantern, 1950s, molded by Tico Toys/Rosbro, not marked, 5" x 4" , orange plastic, black and white paint. (*Courtesy of Dave and Ginny Wellington.*) $65-85.

Orange and black cat with whiskers, 1950s, molded by Tico Toys/Rosbro, not marked, 3.5" x 3", orange and black plastic, black painted eyes and whiskers. (*Courtesy of Mark and Judy Craven.*) $40-50.

Black donkey on wheels, jack-o'-lantern in mouth, early 1950s, molded by Tico Toys/Rosbro, not marked, 5.5" x 5", black plastic, orange paint, orange wheels, fragile toy. (*Courtesy of Dave and Ginny Wellington.*) $150-175.

Orange donkey on wheels, jack-o'-lantern in mouth, early 1950s, molded by Tico Toys/Rosbro, not marked, 5.5" x 5", orange plastic, black paint, black wheels, fragile toy. (*Courtesy of Dave and Ginny Wellington.*) $150-175.

Close-up of original tag on Easter donkey on wheels. (*Author's collection.*)

Easter donkey on wheels, holiday crossover candy container, early 1950s, molded by Tico Toys/Rosbro, not marked, 5.5" x 5", yellow plastic, green paint, green wheels, fragile toy. (*Author's Collection.*) $135-165.

Witch with jack-o'-lantern, painted face, early 1950s, embossed "Rosbro Plastics, Providence, Rhode Island," 3.75" x 2.5", orange plastic, black, red, white, and flesh-color paint. (*Author's collection.*) $35-55.

Selection of other flesh-colored, Rosbro-molded candy containers. These pieces are older than other Rosen pieces. These could also be Tico Toys pieces. (*Author's collection.*)

Clear witch with jack-o'-lantern, original candy, 1950s, embossed "Rosbro Plastics, Providence, Rhode Island, " 3.75" x 2.5", clear plastic, black paint. (*Courtesy of Mark and Judy Craven.*) $35-45.

Witch with jack-o'-lantern on wheels, early 1950s, embossed "Rosbro Plastics, Providence Rhode Island, " 4.75" x 2.75", orange plastic, black paint, black platform, orange wheels. (*Courtesy Mark and Judy Craven.*) $50-65.

Witch with jack-o'-lantern, original cellophane, 1950s, embossed "Rosbro Plastics, Providence, Rhode Island, " 3.75" x 2.5", orange plastic, black paint. (*Courtesy of Richard Miller.*) $35-45.

Clear and black cat with jack-o'-lantern, 1950s, embossed "Rosbro Plastics, Providence, Rhode Island, " 2.75" x 3.63", clear plastic, black paint. (*Courtesy of Mark and Judy Craven.*) $35-45.

Black and orange cat with jack-o'-lantern, 1950s, embossed "Rosbro Plastics, Providence, Rhode Island, " 2.75" x 3.63", orange plastic, black paint. (*Author's collection.*) $35-45.

Orange and black cat with jack-o'-lantern, 1950s, black inside, embossed "Rosbro Plastics, Providence, Rhode Island, " 2.75" x 3.63", black plastic, orange paint. (*Courtesy of Mark and Judy Craven.*) $35-45.

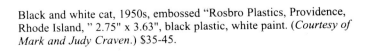

Black and white cat, 1950s, embossed "Rosbro Plastics, Providence, Rhode Island, " 2.75" x 3.63", black plastic, white paint. (*Courtesy of Mark and Judy Craven.*) $35-45.

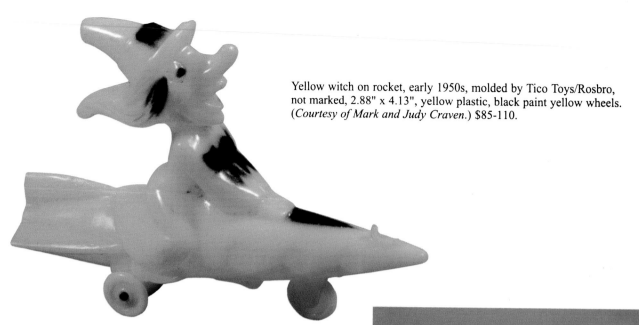

Yellow witch on rocket, early 1950s, molded by Tico Toys/Rosbro, not marked, 2.88" x 4.13", yellow plastic, black paint yellow wheels. (*Courtesy of Mark and Judy Craven.*) $85-110.

Orange witch on rocket, early 1950s, molded by Tico Toys/Rosbro, not marked, 2.88" x 4.13", orange plastic, black paint, yellow wheels. (*Courtesy of Dave and Ginny Wellington.*) $85-110.

Orange witch on rocket, yellow movable back wheels and orange fixed front wheel, early 1950s, molded by Tico Toys/Rosbro, not marked, 2.88" x 4.13", orange plastic, black paint. (*Courtesy of Mark and Judy Craven.*) $85-110.

Three small jack-o'-lantern candy containers, 1950s, molded by Tico Toys/Rosbro, not marked, 2.38" x 2.5", orange and black plastic, tilted tops, different color combinations. (*Courtesy of Mark and Judy Craven.*) $25-35.

Snowman with white hat and pipe, 1950, embossed "Rosbro Plastics, Providence, Rhode Island, " 5.13" x 2.75", orange plastic, black paint. (*Courtesy of Mark and Judy Craven.*) $65-95.

Snowman in black hat with skull and crossbones, black pipe, 1950s, embossed "Rosbro Plastics, Providence Rhode Island," 5.13" x 2.75", orange plastic, black and white paint. (*Courtesy of Tana DeRenzo.*) $65-95.

Snowman white hat with skull and cross bones and white pipe, 1950s, embossed "Rosbro Plastics, Providence, Rhode Island, " 5.13" x 2.75", orange plastic, black paint. (*Courtesy of Mark and Judy Craven.*) $65-95.

Snowman black hat and black pipe, 1950s, embossed "Rosbro Plastics, Providence, Rhode Island, " 5.13" x 2.75", orange plastic, black paint. (*Author's collection.*) $65-95.

Boxed E. Rosen circus, 1950s, includes Trojan horse on wheels, snowman, witch on wheels, and clown on wheels. All toys are embossed "Rosbro Plastics, Providence, Rhode Island." Box is from "E. Rosen Company, Providence, Rhode Island." A good example of Rosbro and E. Rosen being the same company. (*Courtesy of Mark and Judy Craven.*)

E. Rosen box with toys in front. (*Courtesy of Mark and Judy Craven.*) $450-600.

Side of boxed Halloween circus.

Tico Toys Easter basket, 1940s, contains Easter chick on bicycle, pink and yellow plastic, green paint, Tico Toys items were sold in cellophane bags like this. (*Courtesy of Dave and Ginny Wellington.*) $45-55.

Cat sucker holder, original candy, 1950s, molded by Tico Toys/ Rosbro, not marked, 7" x 1.88", orange plastic, black paint. *Courtesy of Dave and Ginny Wellington* $30-45.

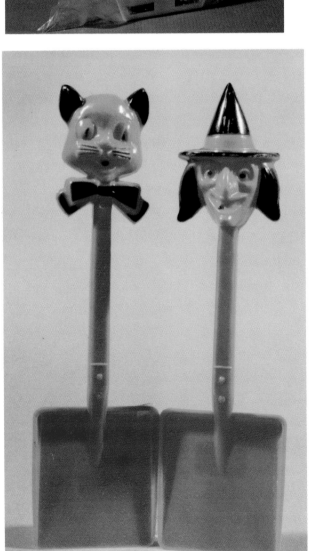

Witch and cat sucker holders, 1950s, molded by Tico Toys/Rosbro, not marked, 7" x 1.88", orange plastic, black paint. (*Courtesy of Mark and Judy Craven.*) $25-35 each.

E. Rosen Nut Cup, 1950s, embossed "Rosbro Plastics, Providence, Rhode Island, " 3.25" x 3.25", orange plastic, black handle. (*Courtesy of Mark and Judy Craven.*) $10-15.

Jack-o'-lantern with witch and cat, 1950s, molded by Tico Toys/ Rosbro, not marked, no platform, large hole on top for candy, 2.88" x 3.88", orange plastic, black and white paint. (*Courtesy of Mark and Judy Craven.*) $45-60.

Small papier-maché jack-o'-lantern nut cup with hard plastic container. Both are from the same era, late 1940s, early 1950s.

Jack-o'-lantern with witch and cat on platform with handle, 1950s, molded by Tico Toys/Rosbro, not marked, 3.63" x 4", orange plastic, white and black paint, green platform, yellow wheels, yellow handle. (*Courtesy of Mark and Judy Craven.*) $65-75.

Jack-o'-lantern with witch and cat, large hole for candy, 1950s, molded by Tico Toys/Rosbro, not marked, 2.88" x 3.88", orange plastic, black paint. (*Courtesy of Mark and Judy Craven.*) $45-60.

Jack-o'-lantern with witch and cat, small hole for sucker, 1950s, molded by Tico Toys/Rosbro, not marked, 2.88" x 3.88", orange plastic, black paint, black base. (*Courtesy of Mark and Judy Craven.*) $45-50.

Jack-o'-lantern with witch and cat, small hole for sucker, 1950s, molded by Tico Toys/Rosbro, not marked, 2.88" x 3.88", orange and black plastic, white paint, white base. (*Courtesy of Mark and Judy Craven.*) $45-60.

Jack-o'-lantern with witch and cat, small hole for sucker, 1950s, molded by Tico Toys/Rosbro, not marked, 2.88" x 3.88", black and orange plastic with white paint. (*Courtesy of Mark and Judy Craven.*) $45-50.

Jack-o'-lantern with witch and cat, small hole for sucker, 1950s, molded by Tico Toys/Rosbro, not marked, 2.88" x 3.88", orange and black plastic, black paint, black base. (*Courtesy of Mark and Judy Craven.*) $45-50.

Jack-o'-lantern with witch and cat, small hole for sucker, 1950s, molded by Tico Toys/Rosbro, not marked, 2.88" x 3.88", all orange plastic, eyes cut out. (*Courtesy of Mark and Judy Craven.*) $45-55.

Witch on motorcycle, flat, sucker holder, late 1940s, molded by Tico Toys/Rosbro, not marked, 4.63" x 2.63", orange plastic, black paint. (*Courtesy of Mark and Judy Craven.*) $25-35.

Jack-o'-lantern with witch and cat, small hole for sucker, 1950s, molded by Tico Toys/Rosbro, not marked, 2.88" x 3.88", all yellow plastic, eyes cut out, 10-cent price tag on top. (*Courtesy of Mark and Judy Craven.*) $45-55.

Jazz cat with jack-o'-lantern, flat, sucker holder, late 1940s, molded by Tico Toys/ Rosbro, not marked, 4.75" x 2.38", orange plastic, black paint. (*Courtesy of Mark and Judy Craven.*) $25-35.

Small E. Rosen candy containers, not marked, 2" x 1.5", these were tied to or inside cellophane stuffed with candy or suckers from the factory. (*Author's collection.*) $15-18.

Witch hat, late 1960s transitional piece. The composition of plastic has changed to a more durable product similar to early Hong Kong pieces, tagged E. Rosen, Pawtucket, Rhode Island, probably went on a vinyl pumpkin, 4.25" x 4". (*Courtesy of Mark and Judy Craven.*) $15-20. With pumpkin, $35-55.

Trumpet, early 1950s, molded by Tico Toys/Rosbro, not marked, 10.75" x 3.75", orange plastic at both ends. (*Courtesy of Mark and Judy Craven.*) $55-75.

Saxophone, early 1950s, molded by Tico Toys/Rosbro, not marked, 9.75" x 4", black plastic, orange mouth piece. Note: Rosbro molded many types of musical instruments for candy containers. (*Courtesy of Mark and Judy Craven.*) $55-75.

Scarecrow with jack-o'-lantern head, 1950s, molded by Tico Toys/Rosbro, not marked, 5" x 4", orange plastic, black paint. (*Courtesy of Mark and Judy Craven.*) $35-45.

Scarecrow with jack-o'-lantern head, original candy, 1950s, molded by Tico Toys/Rosbro, not marked, tagged E. Rosen Company, 5" x 4", orange plastic, black painted checkered top. (*Courtesy of Dave and Ginny Wellington.*) $35-50.

Scarecrow with jack-o'-lantern head, 1950s, molded by Tico Toys/Rosbro, not marked, 5.75" x 4", orange plastic, black paint, green platform, orange wheels, original tassel. (*Courtesy of Mark and Judy Craven.*) $65-95.

Scarecrow with jack-o'-lantern head on wheels, 1950s, molded by Tico Toys/Rosbro, not marked, 5.75" x 4", orange plastic, black checkered top, green platform, orange wheels, original tassel. (*Courtesy of Mark and Judy Craven.*) $65-95.

Scarecrow with jack-o'-lantern head, 1950s, molded by Tico Toys/Rosbro, not marked, 5.75" x 4", orange plastic, black paint, green platform, green wheels. (*Courtesy of Richard Miller/Photo by Richard Miller.*) $65-95.

Scarecrow with jack-o'-lantern head on top of vinyl pumpkin, 1950s, tagged "E. Rosen Company, Pawtucket, Rhode Island," molded by Rosbro Plastics. A great transitional piece. Scarecrows were used by the E. Rosen company for many years. 9" x 6". (*Courtesy of Mark and Judy Craven.*) $45-55.

Party goer on platform with small jack-o'-lantern, early 1950s, molded by Tico Toys/Rosbro, not marked, 5" x 3", white plastic, red and black paint, green hat, green platform, orange wheels, rare. (*Courtesy of Mark and Judy Craven.*) $175-200.

Party goers on platforms with small jack-o'-lanterns, early 1950s, molded by Tico Toys/Rosbro, not marked, man is 5" x 3", woman is 4.5" x 3" with a replaced jack-o'-lantern, white plastic, red and black paint, black hats, green platform, orange wheels. (*Courtesy of Richard Miller/Photo by Richard Miller.*) Man $175-200, woman $145-165.

Valentine party goer girl on wheels, early 1950s, molded by Tico Toys/Rosbro, 5" x 3". There are most likely Thanksgiving candy containers like this. . (*Courtesy of Richard Miller/Photo by Richard Miller.*) $55-75.

Smoking jack-o'-lantern flat sucker holder, 1950s, molded by Tico Toys/Rosbro, not marked, 4.38" x 2.5", orange plastic, black paint. (*Author's collection.*) $35-45.

Party whistle, dog with mask, 1950s, molded by Tico Toys/Rosbro, not marked, 2.13" x 1.88", orange plastic, black paint. (*Courtesy of Mark and Judy Craven.*) $35-50.

Party whistles: Elephant with mask, orange plastic, black paint; and pig with mask, yellow plastic, black paint; 1950s, molded by Tico Toys/Rosbro. (*Courtesy of Dave and Ginny Wellington.*) $35-50.

Turkey, 1950s, Rosbro style, not marked, 3.5" x 3.5", white plastic with brown, red, and orange paint. (*Courtesy of Dave and Ginny Wellington.*) $35-45.

Party whistle, pig with mask, 1950s, molded by Tico Toys/Rosbro, not marked 2.13" x 1.88", orange plastic, black paint. (*Courtesy of Mark and Judy Craven.*) $35-50.

Monkey finger puppet, E. Rosen Co. Providence, Rhode Island, orange hard-plastic head, 1.5" tall, bottom is thin vinyl 4" x 4" black and orange paint, early 1950s. (*Courtesy of Richard Miller/Photo by Richard Miller.*) $50-65.

Pirate's auto with scarecrow on top, early 1950s, molded by Tico Toys/Rosbro, not marked, 4.5" x 5.13", orange, white, black, and green plastic, black paint, white wheels, very rare. (*Courtesy of Mark and Judy Craven.*) $300-350.

Pirate's auto with cat on top, early 1950s, molded by Tico Toys Toys/Rosbro, not marked, 4.25" x 5.13", orange, green, white, and black plastic, black paint, very rare. (*Courtesy of Mark and Judy Craven.*) $300-350.

Springy head cats on wheels, the boy plays a fiddle, the girl holds a jack-o'-lantern, late 1940s, molded by Tico Toys/Rosbro, not marked, boy 9.25" x 4.5", girl 9" x 4.38", orange plastic, yellow and black paint, bow ties, green wheels, very rare. (*Courtesy of Mark and Judy Craven.*) $350-400.

Novelty bank Halloween clown on wheels, late 1940s, molded by Tico Toy, not marked, 7.5" x 6.75", orange plastic, black and green paint, yellow wheels. (*Courtesy of Mark and Judy Craven.*) $375-450.

Springy head cat on wheels, late 1940s, molded by Tico Toys/Rosbro, not marked, 9.25" x 4.5", yellow plastic, black and green paint, has a fiddle, bow tie missing. (*Courtesy of Dave and Ginny Wellington.*) $300-350.

Clown on wheels, late 1940s, molded by Tico Toy, not marked, 7.5" x 6.75", yellow plastic, red and white paint, novelty clown bank tag, blue wheels. Came in original Tico Toys package. (*Author's collection.*) $375-450.

Chapter Two
Jack-o'-lanterns

Union Products

Union products was the main manufacturer of battery operated lanterns and lights. These were safer for children to carry than papier-mâché lanterns with candles. Union products began in New York under the ownership of George Progin and James Sullivan. The corporation has remained an American-owned business and continues to manufacture products in Leominster, Massachusetts.

Don Featherstone co-owns the corporation now and has gone through many corporate obstacles to keep production in the Leominster area. He designs Halloween molds for the company and his pieces are signed and dated. Mr. Featherstone is an avid collector himself. He redesigned the Union Product witch #305 into a beautiful Halloween lamp that is sure to become a collectors' item.

As we search though flea markets for Union Products jack-o'-lanterns, we find that some have green eyes, some have black eyes, some have wire bails, and some have plastic bails. The green-eyed jack-o'-lanterns with the wire bails are the oldest. There are also black-eyed jack-o'-lanterns with wire bails as well as plastic bails. Some have white pupils and others seem to have painted features with a glow-in-the-dark paint. Be sure your jack-o'-lantern is complete with the battery insert before you pay full price. Without the battery insert it should be half price or less depending on the condition of the plastic.

The Union Products harvest pumpkin shown in this chapter was made for a short period if time. It was not a popular item and was discontinued almost immediately. If you own one of these pumpkins you have a real treasure. There were no samples of the harvest pumpkin to evaluate a price.

Union Products manufactures all holiday items and is famous for plastic pink flamingos, which are sold at the National Plastics Museum in Leominster, Massachusetts.

The Miller Electric Company and Rosbro Plastics

Rosbro Plastics of Providence, Rhode Island, molded jack-o'-lanterns that were electrified or made battery operated by the Miller Electric Company. Their battery insert is on top of the lantern and the eyes are diamond shaped with white pupils. All of these jack-o'-lanterns have wire bails. The Miller Electric Company electrified many other holiday items molded by Rosbro Plastics Providence, Rhode Island.

Union Product jack-o'-lantern #95, wire bail, early 1950s, orange plastic, green eyes, battery operated lantern, 3.38" x 4". (*Courtesy of Mark and Judy Craven.*) $45-65.

Union Products jack-o'-lantern #95, wire bail, early 1950s, orange plastic, black and white eyes, nose and teeth, battery operated lantern, 3.38" x 4". (*Courtesy of Mark and Judy Craven.*) $45-65. Electrified version #95E $55-85.

Missing battery insert and the original 39-cent price tag, Union Products jack-o'-lantern #99.

Union Products jack-o'-lantern #95, wire bail, early 1950s, orange plastic, black painted eyes, battery operated lantern, bottom battery insert missing, 3.38" x 4". (*Courtesy of Mark and Judy Craven.*) $20-45.

Union Products jack-o'-lantern #99, wire bail, 1950s, orange plastic, black and white painted teeth and mouth, battery operated lantern, 5.25" x 6". (*Courtesy Of Mark and Judy Craven.*) $65-85. Electrified version #99E $85-100.

Union Products Trick or Treat jack-o'-lantern #97, 1950s, happy treat face, frowning trick face on other side, orange plastic, large black plastic handle, candy container, rare. 5.5" x 8". (*Courtesy of John and Virginia Punashot.*) $200-275. Electrified version #97E $250-325.

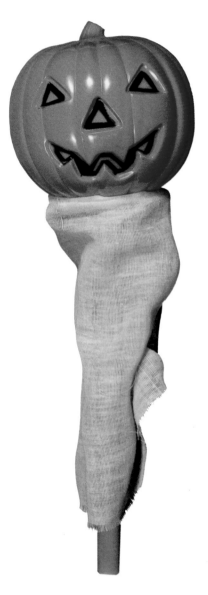

Other side of Trick or Treat jack-o'-lantern. (*Courtesy of John and Virginia Punashot.*)

Union Products jack-o'-lantern on a Stick, #89 jack-o'-lantern , 1960s, orange plastic, black painted eyes, cloth covering stick, battery operated lantern, 3.5" lantern on 10" stick. (*Courtesy of Mark and Judy Craven.*) $55-75.

Union Products jack-o'-lantern #90, 1950s, wire bail, orange plastic, black and white paint, green painted stem, battery operated, 3.5" x 4". (*Courtesy of Mark and Judy Craven.*) $35-50.

Comparison photo of Pulpco Co. of Milwaukee jack-o'-lantern on left, 1950s, and Union Products' pail on right, 3.5" x 4", wire bails. (*Courtesy of Mark and Judy Craven.*)

Union Products Favor jack-o'-lantern #91 left, 1950s, Rosbro small jack-o'-lantern right, orange plastic, black paint candy containers, left 1.88" x 2.5", right 1.63" x 1.38". (*Courtesy of Mark and Judy Craven.*) Left $15-20, right $5-10.

Union Products Candy jack-o'-lantern #98, 1950s, scalloped-top orange plastic pail with plastic bail, black paint, 3.5" x 5". (*Author's Collection*) $25-45.

Union Products battery operated jack-0'-lanterns with plastic bails, #90 on left, #99 on right, 1960s, orange plastic with black paint. Left 3.5" x 4"; right 6" x 5.25". (*Author's collection.*) Left $25-45, right $55-65.

Union Products brochure, 1952. (*Courtesy of Don Featherstone.*)

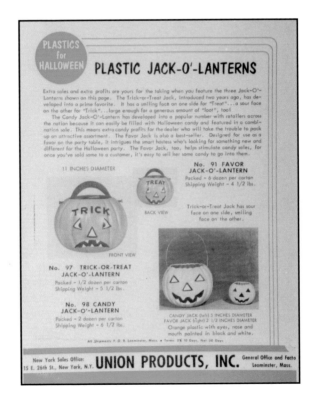

Union Products brochure, Trick or Treat jack-o'-lantern, early 1950s. (*Courtesy of Don Featherstone.*)

Union Products brochure, electrified jack-o'-lanterns, 1950s, #97E Trick or Treat jack-o'-lantern. (*Courtesy of Don Featherstone.*)

Union Products brochure, Harvest Pumpkin 1950s. (*Courtesy of Don Featherstone.*)

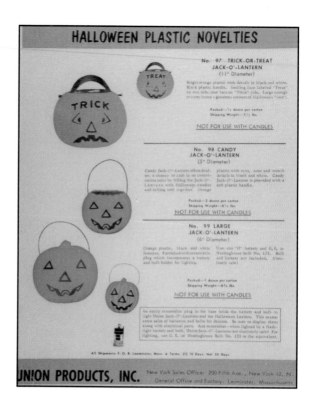

Union Products Halloween brochure, Plastic Novelties 1950s. (*Courtesy of Don Featherstone.*)

Union Products Halloween brochure, Plastic Novelties 1950s. (*Courtesy of Don Featherstone.*)

Union Products brochure, 1962. (*Courtesy of Don Featherstone.*)

Union Products jagged-mouth jack-o'-lantern, early 1950s, cut-out features, orange plastic, black paint, early wire bail, battery operated lantern, 3.5" x 3.75". (*Courtesy Of Mark and Judy Craven.*) $65-85.

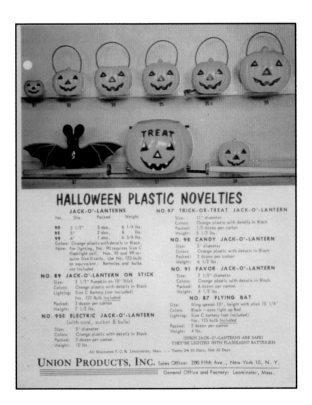

Union Products brochure, Halloween Plastics Novelties 1962. (*Courtesy of Don Featherstone.*)

Pulpco Co. Milwaukee, Wisconsin, 1950s, battery operated lantern, orange plastic, black and white paint, green top battery insert, 4.5" x 4.75", rare. (*Courtesy of Mark and Judy Craven.*) $65-85.

Miller Electric Co. electrified Rosbro jack-o'-lantern, late 1940s, orange plastic, diamond-shaped eyes, battery operated, battery insert on top, black and white paint, boxed lantern. 4" x 4.88". (*Courtesy of Ann and Rich Davidson/Photo by Richard Miller.*) $85-120.

Miller Electric Co. boxed jack-o'-lantern, left, and boxed snowman, right, molded by Rosbro Plastics, Providence, Rhode Island. (*Courtesy of Richard Miller/Photo by Richard Miller.*)

Boxed battery operated jack-o'-lantern, transitional piece, orange celluloid head, orange and black hard-plastic hands and feet, black and white paint, metal base, early 1940s. The box is 4" x 2" the jack-o'-lantern is 5" x 4". (*Courtesy of Richard Miller/Photo by Richard Miller.*)

Shy jack-o'-lantern with wire bail, 1950s, not marked, hard orange plastic, white and black paint, 3.63" x 5". (*Courtesy of Mark and Judy Craven.*) $45-55.

Rosbro battery operated jack-o'-lantern on wheels by Miller Electric Co., late 1940s, orange plastic, black and white paint, green platform with yellow wheels, original tassel, 5.5" x 6", rare. (*Courtesy of Mark and Judy Craven.*) $150-200.

Hard plastic 1950s jack-o'-lantern, not marked, 5.5" x 5", orange plastic, black paint. (*Courtesy of George and Cindy Grew.*) $55-75.

Jack-o'-lantern with crown, candy container, late 1940s into the 1950s, molded by Tico Toys/Rosbro, orange plastic, black paint, wire bail, 3.5" x 4.5". (*Author's collection.*) $45-65.

Jack-o'-lantern with crown and chalk jack-o'-lantern from the same era. (*Author's collection.*)

Transitional vinyl jack-o'-lantern with wire bail, 1960s, not marked, orange vinyl, black and white paint, 4" x 4.75". (*Author's collection.*) $10-15.

Three diamond-eyed jack-o'-lanterns, 1940s, 1960s, 1990s. All are unmarked. (*Author's collection.*)

Large plastic-head witch with broom, life size. (*Courtesy of Mark and Judy Craven.*)

Belindy with older Halloween candy containers, lanterns, and hard plastic clown. (*Author's collection.*)

"Andy do you think he is related to us? He does have the same family nose." (*Author's collection.*)

Chapter Three

Others Made in the U.S.A.

Items from the 1940s to Early 1960s

The Best Plastics Corp. in Brooklyn, New York, made hard plastic novelties for the holidays and parties in the late 1940s. Their products were of good quality and design. There is another Best Novelty Co. now in Brooklyn, New York, that is related to the early toy novelty company, however it only distributes novelties and doesn't manufacture them.

Lapin was a company started in 1912 by Max Rosenfield. Lapin started by producing notions and novelties in Catalin. Lapin began to use injection molding in 1936 and continued into the hard plastic era. These items are rare and hard to find. Around 1943 the products are embossed, "A Lapin Product Newark 5, N.J." The United States adopted the first area numbering in mid-1943, a predecessor to our present zip codes which came about in 1963. This company's last address was 164 Delany Street, Newark, New Jersey 1950.

Commonwealth Plastics was started in Leomister, Massachusetts, by Bill Lester. He was a pioneer in the plastics industry for a long time. Commonwealth molded toys and novelties in hard plastic from the late 1940s. Their products were featured as favors at birthday parties, as well as the holidays. They were of excellent quality.

Fun World Inc.

Fun World Inc. began in the early 1960s. They make toys for all holidays. The plastic composition varied through the years. The earliest Fun World Inc. toys are made and embossed "Hong Kong" without a zip code. Each toy is embossed differently. Fun World Inc. or Easter Unlimited is located in Carle Place, New York, and is under the direction of Stanley Geller, who was amazed to see these products becoming collector items.

Many items were repeated by Fun World Inc. throughout the years. You can find the same items embossed "Hong Kong," and later "China" with a five-digit zip code. Hong Kong Fun World Inc. items were made until the mid 1980s when production shifted to China. In China there was not a clear copyright understanding with the United States. They didn't always remove the Hong Kong mold mark, therefore some items have "Hong Kong" on them when they really have been made in China. Many American toy companies have had to deal with this same issue and the United States government has been working with all overseas governments to straighten out our copyright and licensing laws. You can look for the earliest Fun World Inc. to collect or go ahead and explore the newer collectibles. Remember it is all in fun.

Miniatures Made in Hong Kong and China

Some of the same cake-top decorations and small-candy containers have been made in Hong Kong or China up to the present time. These newer pieces have very rough mold marks, the items are smaller and are vinylized so they bend easily. The artwork in the faces is not as good. The older Hong Kong pieces are of better quality than the Hong Kong or China pieces of today, although new computer imaging is making the items produced today look better. Labor cost, material costs, and general production costs have forced producers to use thinner material and less design. The collector should become familiar with the quality between old Hong Kong and new Hong Kong and China before you purchase an item.(See photographs that show plastic quality on Page 81.)

Union Products Witch #305, early 1950s, company records show this witch was made for only a few years ending in 1954, 5.25" x 5.13", orange plastic with black paint. (*Author's collection*.) $250-300. Electrified version #305E $300-325.

Union Products 1952 brochure for witch #305. (*Courtesy of Don Featherstone.*)

Union Products brochure 1952 for witch #305E. (*Courtesy of Don Featherstone.*)

Union Products 1950s brochure for a Gay plastic jack-o'-lantern and witch #305. (*Courtesy of Don Featherstone.*)

Kokomold Pumpkin coach from Kokomold Inc., Kokomo, Indiana. Witch driving a pumpkin being pulled by a black cat, 5.25" x 9.38", orange plastic, black and white paint, black pumpkin wheels on metal axles. (*Courtesy of Tana DeRenzo.*) $350-400.

Union Products #92 lantern with battery insert, 1950s, 8" x 4.5". black plastic with orange paper panel, wire bail. (*Courtesy of George and Cindy Grew.*) $85-125. #92E electrified $90-135.

Union Products 1950s brochure for #92 and 92E Halloween Lantern. *Courtesy of Don Featherstone.*

PLASTICS for HALLOWEEN

HALLOWEEN LANTERN

The Halloween Lantern is a newcomer to the Union line this year. Available in two styles - lighted with flashlight battery and bulb for carrying or wired for use on standard 110-volt household current - it is a versatile Halloween number.

Made of durable black plastic and equipped with a wire handle, the Halloween Lantern is sturdily built. When lighted, each of the four panels shows a different appropriate design silhouetted against an orange panel. The youngsters will delight in carrying the battery-lighted number while the one wired for household lighting systems has a wide range of decorative uses at Halloween. It's ideal for use as a lighted decoration in a window or on a hall table and it's equally appropriate as a centerpiece on the Halloween party table.

Dealers will want to feature it prominently in their Halloween displays, for besides its appeal to the kiddies, it offers a chance to make extra sales of flashlight batteries and bulbs.

No. 92 HALLOWEEN LANTERN

Packed - 1 dozen per carton
Shipping Weight - 4 3/4 lbs.

The Lantern designed for lighting with flashlight battery and bulb is equipped with an ingenious switch so it can be turned on or off without removing the plug in the bottom. Equipped with poylethylene plug that won't work loose.

No. 92E ELECTRIC HALLOWEEN LANERN

Complete with approved cord set and bulb.
Packed - 1 dozen per carton
Shipping Weight - 5 1/2 lbs.

SIZE: 4 1/2" x 4 1/2" x 8" high
COLORS: Black Plastic Silhouettes on Orange Colored Panel

New York Sales Office: E. 26th St., New York, N.Y.
UNION PRODUCTS, INC.
General Office and Factory Leominster, Mass.

All Shipments F. O. B. Leominster, Mass. • Terms: 2% 10 Days, Net 30 Days

Kokomold tag, front. (*Courtesy of Mark and Judy Craven.*)

Kokomold pumpkin coach, wrong wheels, $150-200.

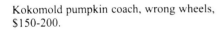

Kokomold tag, back. (*Courtesy of Mark and Judy Craven.*)

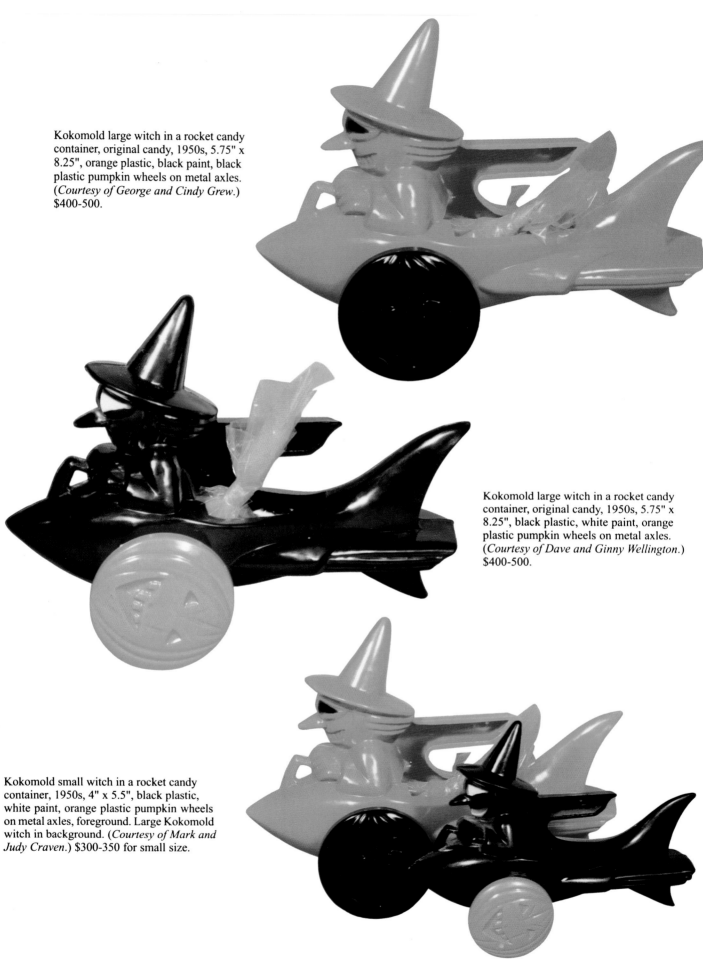

Kokomold large witch in a rocket candy container, original candy, 1950s, 5.75" x 8.25", orange plastic, black paint, black plastic pumpkin wheels on metal axles. (*Courtesy of George and Cindy Grew.*) $400-500.

Kokomold large witch in a rocket candy container, original candy, 1950s, 5.75" x 8.25", black plastic, white paint, orange plastic pumpkin wheels on metal axles. (*Courtesy of Dave and Ginny Wellington.*) $400-500.

Kokomold small witch in a rocket candy container, 1950s, 4" x 5.5", black plastic, white paint, orange plastic pumpkin wheels on metal axles, foreground. Large Kokomold witch in background. (*Courtesy of Mark and Judy Craven.*) $300-350 for small size.

Kokomold small witch in a rocket candy container, 1950s, 4" x 5.5" orange plastic, black paint, black plastic pumpkin wheels on metal axles, foreground. Large Kokomold witch in background. (*Courtesy of Dave and Ginny Wellington.*) $300-350 for small size.

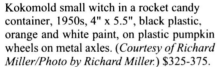

Kokomold small witch in a rocket candy container, 1950s, 4" x 5.5", black plastic, orange and white paint, on plastic pumpkin wheels on metal axles. (*Courtesy of Richard Miller/Photo by Richard Miller.*) $325-375.

Union Products bat (see Union Products brochure photo on Page 47), 1960s, had one cell battery, on a stick, discontinued because it was not child safe. Wing spread 10", height 15.25" with stick, black plastic bat, vinyl wings, red paint. Eyes would light up red. (*Courtesy of Mark and Judy Craven.*) $135-150; $50-60 without original stick and battery holder.

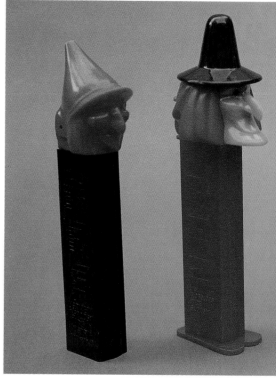

Jack-o'-lantern battery operated lantern, 1950s, marked "Pigeon AAA," made in Japan, 1950s, 59 cents at Woolworth's, original price tag, box 3.88" x 2.75", metal bottom painted black with orange plastic globe painted black and white. (*Courtesy of Richard Miller.*) $85-110.

Pez candy containers, the one on the far left is from the 1950s, others are from the 1990s. (*Author's collection.*) Left to right: $125, $5-7, $5-7, $5-7.

Western Gun, 1950s, 2.50" x 5.38", not marked, orange plastic with an embossed picture of a Ranger. (*Courtesy of Dave and Ginny Wellington.*) $45-60.

Hard plastic owl whistles, not marked, 1950s, 4" tall, good quality plastic. $45-65 each. (*Courtesy of Richard Miller/Photo by Richard Miller.*)

Halloween party nut cup with witch handle, 1950s, Best Plastics Corporation, Brooklyn, New York, 2.75" x 3.25", orange and black plastic, rectangular shaped. (*Courtesy of Mark and Judy Craven.*) $10-15.

Halloween party nut cup with witch handle, 1950s, Best Plastics Corporation, Brooklyn, New York, 3" x 3.25", orange and black plastic. (*Courtesy of Mark and Judy Craven.*) $10-15.

Nut cups that were used during the same era. (*Author's collection.*)

Halloween party nut cups with jack-o'-lantern faces, 1950s, Windtrob and Sons, Canada Limited, 3" x 2.88", orange and black plastic, clear plastic handles, very delicate. (*Courtesy of Dave and Ginny Wellington.*) $10-20 each.

Halloween Pig bank, 1950s-'60s, West Land Plastic, Newberry Park, California, 4.25" x 6.63", orange plastic, black paint, hat comes off when you put money in. (*Courtesy of Dave and Ginny Wellington.*) $35-50.

Rosen plastic train, used for all occasions, late 1950s, 3.50" x 2", transparent hard plastic, $20-35.

Plastic key wind walker, Durham Industries, made in Japan, 1960s, 6.25" x 3.50", orange and black plastic, cutout features, metal key, early 1960s. (*Courtesy of Mark and Judy Craven.*) $75-90.

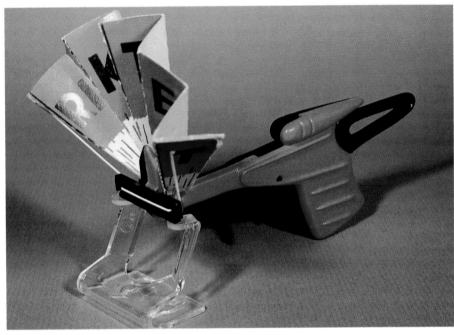

Trick or Treat space gun, 1950s, not marked, 6" x 6.75", back plastic, cardboard insert that springs open to say trick or treat when you shoot gun. (*Courtesy of Randy Pinkerton.*) $100-125.

Front picture of cardboard insert for Halloween space gun,

Tambourine, embossed "Lapin Products, Newark 5, New Jersey," early 1950s, 6" x 1.5", orange and black plastic, orange face. (*Author's collection.*) $125-155.

Halloween horns, all embossed, a Spec Toy product U.S.A., late 1940s, saxophone 6.25" x 4", or in middle 6.38" x 2.38", Trumpet 6.5" x 2.63", orange and black plastic. (*Courtesy of Mark and Judy Craven.*) $45-65 each.

Tambourine, embossed "Lapin Products, Newark 5, New Jersey," early 1950s, 6" x 1.5", orange and black plastic, black face. (*Courtesy of Mark and Judy Craven.*) $125-155.

Small candy container horns made by various companies in the 1950s, orange and black plastic. Left to right: 4.38" x .63", 3.75" x .5", 3.63" x 1.75", 3.5" x 1.88". (*Courtesy of Mark and Judy Craven.*) $10-15 each.

Halloween horn candy stick, tagged "Rudley Products, New York," 1950s, 15"; and saxophone 13", orange and black plastic, original candy. (*Courtesy of Dave and Ginny Wellington.*) $35-45.

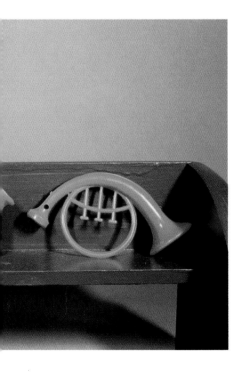

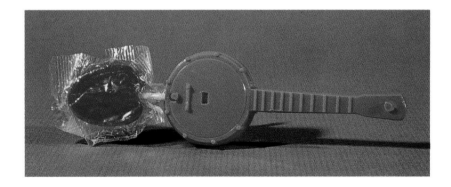

Banjo sucker holder, 1950s, not marked, made in U.S.A., 4.25" x 1.5", orange plastic. (*Courtesy of Dave and Ginny Wellington.*) $10-15.

Halloween cat baby rattle, 1950s, not marked, made in U.S.A., 5" long, orange plastic, white paint, 1950s. (*Courtesy of Dave and Ginny Wellington.*) $45-60.

Halloween jewelry, 1950s, blinky eye jack-o'-lantern on original card, made in U.S.A., 3.5" x 2.88", orange plastic, blinking black eyes. (*Courtesy of Mark and Judy Craven.*) $35-50.

Halloween jewelry, 1950s, blinky eyed devil on original card, 1950s made in U.S.A., 3.5" x 2.38", orange plastic, black paint and blinking eyes. (*Courtesy of Mark and Judy Craven.*) $35-50.

Jack-o'-lantern lantern, hard plastic with a wire handle, 1950s-'60s, Banner U.S.A., 9.25" x 5.5". (*Courtesy of Mark and Judy Craven.*) $125-155.

Broach pin, battery operated light, 1950s, EJ Kahn Company of Chicago, 1950s, 3.38" x 1.5", green, orange and brown plastic. (*Courtesy of Mark and Judy Craven.*) $35-50.

Halloween jewelry, 1950s, blinky eyed owl on original card, 1950s made in U.S.A., 3.5 x 2.75", orange plastic, black paint and blinking eyes. (*Author's collection.*) $35-50.

Celluloid owl ring with bell, 1930s made in U.S.A., 1.75" x 1.13", orange and black celluloid, metal ring and bell. (*Courtesy of Mark and Judy Craven.*) $150-185.

Favorite celluloid novelty dolls, 1930s-1940s. (*Author's collection.*)

Halloween jewelry, 1950s, left blinking eyed witch, 2.25" x 1.13", orange plastic, black and white paint, made in the U.S.A., 1950s, right celluloid jack-o'-lantern with cat, 1.25" x 2", black and orange celluloid, made in U.S.A. 1930s. (*Courtesy of Mark and Judy Craven.*) Left $35-45, right $65-85.

Celluloid jewelry, made in U.S.A. 1930s, 2.38" x 1.88", orange celluloid, black and white paint, cutout features. This jewelry style can also be found in hard plastic. (*Courtesy of Mark and Judy Craven.*) $60-85.

Halloween whistle with two jack-o'-lanterns by Rosbro, whistle marked "Roy Goniea special," 1950s, whistle is orange and black plastic with metal ring. Jack-o'-lanterns 1.63" x 1.25". (*Courtesy of Mark and Judy Craven.*) Whistle $25-35, jack-o'-lanterns $10-15 each.

Sucker holders, made in U.S.A. 1950s, 3.5" x 1.5", orange, white, and black plastic on green platforms. (*Courtesy of Mark and Judy Craven.*) $25-35 each

Sucker holders, made in U.S.A.1950s, 3.50" x 1.5", black, orange, and white plastic on orange and yellow platforms. (*Courtesy of Dave and Ginny Wellington.*) $25-35 each.

Plastic and tin sparkler, marked Japan 1960s, 5" x 2.75", orange and black plastic, lithographed spiders on tin sparkler. (*Courtesy of Mark and Judy Craven.*) $25-40.

Clown clacker candy stick, made in Hong Kong, early 1960s, 5.75" x 14.75", orange and black plastic, with original candy. (*Courtesy of Mark and Judy Craven.*) $45-65.

Clown clacker whistle, not marked, made in U.S.A., Rosbro quality, 5.75" x 6.75", late 1950s, black and orange plastic. (*Courtesy of Mark and Judy Craven.*) $55-85.

Scarecrow game box top, W.H. Schaper Mfg. Minneapolis, Minnesota, 10.25" x 10.25". (*Courtesy of Mark and Judy Craven.*)

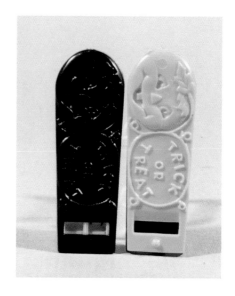

Trick or treat whistles, 1950s, not marked, 2.5" x .78", black and orange plastic. (*Courtesy of Mark and Judy Craven.*) $15-25 each.

Scarecrow game, W.H. Schaper Mfg. Minneapolis, Minnesota, green, yellow, blue, and red plastic 1950s. (*Courtesy of Mark and Judy Craven.*) $45-65.

Magic hat for Easter, Commonwealth Plastics Corporation, Loeminster, Massachusetts, late 1940s, 3" x 3", blue and white plastic. (*Author's collection.*) $45-65.

Buster Brown magic hat for all occasions. (*Author's collection*.) $65-95.

Bottom of Buster Brown hat. There is also a Halloween magic hat.

Black skeleton glasses, Foster Grant, made in the U.S.A. 1950s, 6.50"
x 3.38", black and white plastic. (*Courtesy of Mark and Judy
Craven.*) $55-75.

Jack-o'-lantern with witch glasses, Foster Grant, made in the U.S.A., 1950s, 6" x 3.25", black and orange plastic, yellow paint. (*Courtesy of Mark and Judy Craven.*) $55-75.

Jack-o'-lantern and witch glasses, Foster Grant, made in the U.S.A. 1950s, 6.25" x 3.25", orange and black plastic, black paint. (*Courtesy of Mark and Judy Craven.*) $55-75.

Elgee Disguise set glasses #4320, made in Hong Kong, 1960s, same as Foster Grant. $35-55. (*Courtesy of Richard Miller/Photo by Richard Miller.*)

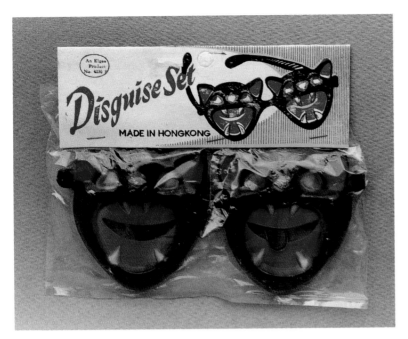

Cat with fangs glasses, Foster Grant, made in U.S.A., 6.25" x 3.25" 1960s, black plastic, red and white paint. (*Courtesy of Mark and Judy Craven.*) $35-55.

Bat glasses, Foster Grant, made in the U.S.A. 1950s, 6.5" x 3.38", white plastic, red and black paint. (*Courtesy of Mark and Judy Craven.*) $55-85.

Witch on motorcycle, Hong Kong #831, K.T. in circle, Rosbro style, 1960s, 3.13" x 1.75", orange plastic, black, green, and silver paint. (*Courtesy of Mark and Judy Craven.*) $15-25.

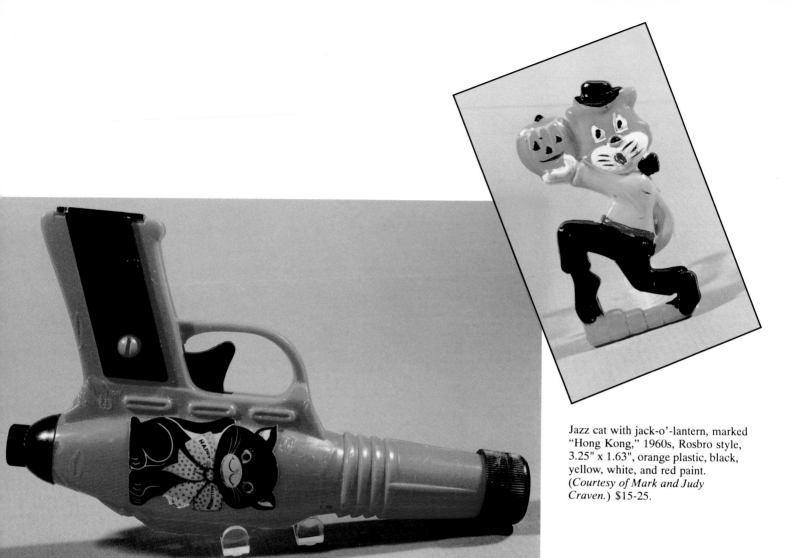

Jazz cat with jack-o'-lantern, marked "Hong Kong," 1960s, Rosbro style, 3.25" x 1.63", orange plastic, black, yellow, white, and red paint. (*Courtesy of Mark and Judy Craven.*) $15-25.

Flashlight gun, made in Hong Kong, 1960s, 6.38" x 3.88", orange and black plastic, with cat on barrel. (*Courtesy of Mark and Judy Craven.*) $35-55.

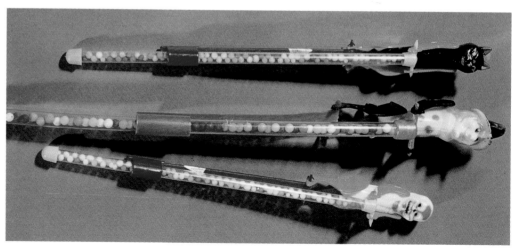

Cat, witch, and skeleton candy sticks, made in Hong Kong, 1960s, cat 9", witch 14.5"and, skeleton 9", white, black, and orange plastic, with original candy. (*Courtesy of Dave and Ginny Wellington.*) $15-25 each.

Halloween camera, Commonwealth Plastic Corporation, U.S.A., late 1940s, 1.5" x 1.5", black plastic with white plastic head coming out of camera. (*Courtesy of Mark and Judy Craven.*) $45-65.

Fun World, ghost and witch coming out of jack-o'-lanterns, pat. #9352, made in Hong Kong, early 1960s, 3.88" x 2", painted plastic, orange, white, green, red, and flesh-color. (*Courtesy of Mark and Judy Craven.*) $25-35 each.

Party hat favor, not marked, made in the U.S.A., 1.5" x 4", 1950s, orange plastic. (*Courtesy of Mark and Judy Craven.*) $15-25.

Halloween baby rattle, Stahlwood Toy Mfg. early 1960s, 3.75" x 2.5", orange plastic, red, white, yellow, black, and flesh-color paint. (*Courtesy of Mark and Judy Craven.*) $25-35.

Fun World walkers, made in Hong Kong, pat. #9357, 2.75" x 2.5", orange plastic, black and green paint, early 1960s. (*Courtesy of Mark and Judy Craven.*) $45-65.

Fun World Halloween flying witch, made in Hong Kong, 6" x 3", orange and black plastic, flesh-color paint, early 1960s. (*Courtesy of Mark and Judy Craven.*) $55-65.

Fun World Halloween flying witch, mint on card, made in Hong Kong, 9.88" x 5", green and black plastic, flesh-color, early 1960s. (*Courtesy of Mark and Judy Craven.*) $65-85.

Fun World cat coming out of jack-o'-lantern, made in Hong Kong, 4.75" x 3.25", early 1960s, orange and black plastic, pink and green paint, winds up on side. (*Courtesy of Mark and Judy Craven.*) $40-55.

Fun World pipe, made in Hong Kong, 1.75" x 5.25", early 1960s, orange plastic, black paint. (*Courtesy of Mark and Judy Craven.*) $15-25.

Fun World cat on rollers, made in Hong Kong, 3.75" x 2.25", early 1960s, black and orange plastic, white, orange, and green paint, jack-o'-lantern rolls around inside of cat. (*Courtesy of Dave and Ginny Wellington.*) $20-35.

Fun World witch on roller, made in Hong Kong, 3.75" x 2.25", early 1960s, black and orange plastic, green, white, and purple paint, jack-o'-lantern rolls around inside of witch. (*Courtesy of Dave and Ginny Wellington.*) $20-35.

Fun World jack-o'-lantern light, made in Hong Kong, 3.25" x 3.13", early 1970s, yellow and orange plastic, black, red, and white paint, the hole in the nose is for the light bulb. (*Courtesy of Mark and Judy Craven.*) $10-15.

Fun World quartet of push puppets, made in Hong Kong, early 1960s, all measure 3.5" x 1.75", orange, black, white, and green plastic, flesh-color paint on witch second from the left; yellow, black, and red paint. (*Courtesy of Mark and Judy Craven.*) $35-55 each.

Fun World springy toys, made in Hong Kong, early 1980s, all measure 4.5" x 2", also marked "Grand Toy, Hong Kong," orange, white, and black plastic, yellow, black, red, and green paint, rubber suctions. (*Courtesy of Mark and Judy Craven.*) $5-7 each.

Fun World springy toys, made in Hong Kong or China, late 1980s, orange, black, white and green plastic, black paint. Left 4" x 1.75", right 3.5" x 2.5". (*Author's collection.*) $5-7.

Fun World witch on left, made in Hong Kong, early 1960s, 2.75" x 1.5", orange plastic, black paint. Funworld jack-o'-lantern with green goblin coming out of the top, made in China 1980s, 2.5" x 2.5", orange plastic, green, black, and yellow paint. Funworld jack-o'-lantern on right with witch hat, made in Hong Kong, early 1960s, 4" x 2", orange plastic, black and white paint. (*Courtesy of Mark and Judy Craven.*) Left $15-25, center $5-10, right $15-25.

Fun World witch sparkler gun, made in Hong Kong, early 1960s, 4.38" x 3.38", black plastic, clear yellow face, red and orange paint, metal trigger. (*Courtesy of Mark and Judy Craven.*) $35-55.

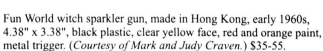

Funworld cat coming out of jack-o'-lantern, New York, made in Hong Kong, no zip code, early 1960s, 3" x 2", orange, black, and green plastic for the stem. (*Author's collection.*) $25-40.

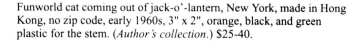

Cake top set, made in Hong Kong, early 1960s, there are nine pieces to this set, orange plastic, black paint. (*Author's collection.*) $15-25.

Cats cake top set, made in Hong Kong early 1960s, 4" x 4", orange plastic, black paint, green and white eyes. (*Author's collection.*) $10-20 each.

Flashlight with mouse coming out of jack-o'-lantern, made in Hong Kong 1960s, 13" x 2.5", orange and black plastic, gray, red, green and black paint, light turns on and off at neck. (*Courtesy of Mark and Judy Craven.*) $25-45.

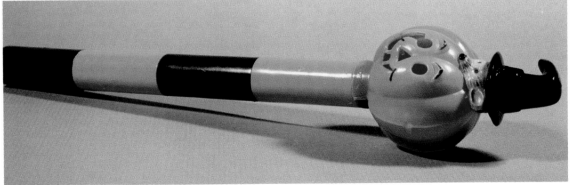

Jack-o'-lantern and cat cake top, made in Hong Kong early 1960s, 4.50" x 3.5", orange plastic, yellow, black, and white paint. This style has been made over the years in various qualities of plastic. (*Author's collection.*) $5-10.

Witches with bats on their shoulders, made in Hong Kong, 1960s. Left 5.25" x 2.38", right 3.38" x 1.63", orange plastic, yellow, white, flesh-color, and black paint. (*Courtesy of Dave and Ginny Wellington.*) Left $20-35, right $10-20.

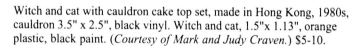

Witch and cat with cauldron cake top set, made in Hong Kong, 1980s, cauldron 3.5" x 2.5", black vinyl. Witch and cat, 1.5"x 1.13", orange plastic, black paint. (*Courtesy of Mark and Judy Craven.*) $5-10.

Large E. Rosen pumpkin man, made in Hong Kong, late 1960s and '70s, "E. Rosen" tag, 7" x 2.5", orange and clear vinyl, with original candy. (*Courtesy of Dave and Ginny Wellington.*) $25-45.

Close up photograph of large E. Rosen pumpkin man tag.

Noise maker, made in Hong Kong, 1960s, 3.75" x 3.5", orange, green plastic, black paint, hat is soft vinyl. (*Courtesy of Mark and Judy Craven.*) $25-45.

Vinyl ghost with pumpkin, embossed "Holland Hall Prod. 1966," 7.75" x 2", white vinyl, orange vinyl jack-o'-lantern, black paint. (*Courtesy of Dave and Ginny Wellington.*) $30-55.

Small cutout hard plastic jack-o'-lantern, Best Plastics Corporation, Brooklyn, New York, zip code 11220, 1960s, 1.75" x 2.25", black and orange plastic. (*Author's collection.*) $10-15.

79

Lite-up pumpkin, Best Toy and Novelty Company, Brooklyn, New York, 1960s, zip code 11220, orange and green soft vinyl, black paint, original 29-cent price tag from Grants Dime Store. (*Author's collection.*) $10-15.

Party decorations, four pieces in original package, 1960s, marked "Made in Hong Kong, Paper Art Company Indianapolis, Indiana 46218," 1- 1.5" tall, orange plastic with black paint. (*Courtesy of Randy Pinkerton.*) $20-30.

Lantern, 1950s, all plastic, not marked, 12" x 5.5", black and orange plastic. (*Courtesy of George and Cindy Grew.*) $150-185.

Small cat candy container in original cellophane wrapper, made in Hong Kong. (*Courtesy of Mark and Judy Craven.*) $10-15.

From left to right: Rosbro, 1950, $15-18; Hong Kong, 1960s, $8-10; Rosbro, 1950s, $15-18; later Hong Kong, $1-2 each. Note the color, size, and design changes through the years. *(Author's collection.)*

From left to right: Hong Kong, 1960s, $8-10; later Hong Kong, $1-2 each, note color size and design through the years. *(Author's collection.)*

New cupcake tops made in Hong Kong, 1980s-1990s. *(Author's collection.)* $1-3.

Newer cupcake tops, made in China with computer imaging for better faces, *(Author's collection.)* $.50-1 each.

Chapter Four

Later Items

Empire Industries Inc.

Empire Industries has produced good quality, hard-vinyl Halloween items since the mid-1960s. Their corporate offices are in Del Ray Beach, Florida. They manufacture products in Tarboro, North Carolina, and also have an office on Fifth Avenue in New York. The most attractive Empire items to collect are the jack-o'-lanterns and the Halloween lamps with the different faces that were made for a short period of time. This company has repeated their basic jack-o'-lantern mold for many years. It is found with many different dates from the late 1960s through the 1990s. You can rescue and recycle many of these at your local thrift stores.

Merry Miniatures, Hallmark, left to right: scarecrow holding jack-o'-lantern, 1974, $280-325; small sitting witch, 1986, $65-90; scarecrow with pumpkin, 1976, $375-450; cat with hat, 1978, $25-30; ghost with corn, 1992, $10-15; owl on jack-o'-lantern, 1976, $200-285; flocked kitten, 1978, $35-50. (*Courtesy of Dave and Ginny Wellington.*)

Hallmark

The Merry Miniatures were first introduced by Hallmark Cards Inc. in 1974. They are made for all major holidays and are used for table decorations, party favors, and gifts. The majority are made of quality plastic and average in size from one to three inches in height. Hallmark designers give each Merry Miniature a personality customers can appreciate. These creative designs make the pieces collector quality.

In the past few years the Merry Miniatures have become very collectible and have risen in value so that they compete with the other Halloween collectibles. The first Merry Miniature issued was a scarecrow with a pumpkin at his feet which sold for a dollar. Today that piece is worth from $350 to $400.

You can still find Merry Miniatures as well as other Hallmark pieces at garage sales, flea markets and ornament shows.

Merry Miniatures, Hallmark, left to right: witch with broom, 1977, $150-175; ghost out of jack-o'-lantern, 1981, $250-275; ghost whistle, late-1970s, $275-300; witch with frog on hat, 1982, $300-350; devil, 1975, $365-425. (*Courtesy of Dave and Ginny Wellington and Randy Pinkerton.*)

Hallmark earrings, made in China, 1990s.
(*Author's collection*.) $3-5 pair.

Fun World cup, made in China, 1980s, 1.5"x
2.88", orange plastic, green and black paint,
diamond-shaped eyes. (*Courtesy of Mark
and Judy Craven*.) $8-10.

Hallmark jack-o'-lantern, 1980s, 3.13" x
4", orange, white, and green plastic,
yellow paint, wind-up toy. (*Author's
collection*.) $5-10.

Fun World cup, made in China, 1980s, 1.38"
x 2.75", orange plastic, green and black paint,
triangle-shaped eyes. (*Courtesy of Mark and
Judy Craven*.) $8-10.

Fun World good quality witch on wheels, made in China, new, 5" x 4", black plastic, white, purple, orange, green, and red paint. (*Courtesy of Dave and Ginny Wellington.*) $5-10.

Fun World jack-o'-lantern pop-outs, ghost, and cats, made in Hong Kong, 1980s, these are in the 1996 Fun World catalog, orange, black, and white plastic, red, green and white paint, newer ones are embossed "Made in China." (*Courtesy of Mark and Judy Craven.*) $3-8.

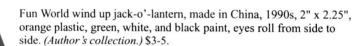

Fun World wind up jack-o'-lantern, made in China, 1990s, 2" x 2.25", orange plastic, green, white, and black paint, eyes roll from side to side. (*Author's collection.*) $3-5.

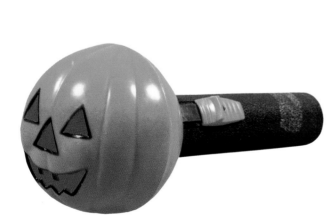

Flashlight, marked "Taiwan," 1980s-1990s, 7.5" x 3.5", orange plastic, handle is foam vinyl, cutout eyes, black paint. (*Courtesy of Mark and Judy Craven*.) $5-10.

Owl and crow nodders, new, not marked, owl 3.25" x 1.5", crow 3.25" x 1.5", brown, black, and orange plastic, with plastic eyes. (*Courtesy of Mark and Judy Craven.*) $10 each.

Blinky brochure, the original Blinky counter display of flashlights. (*Courtesy of Patty Gallagher Magnus.*)

Blinky brochure, party favor containers. (*Courtesy of Patty Gallagher Magnus.*)

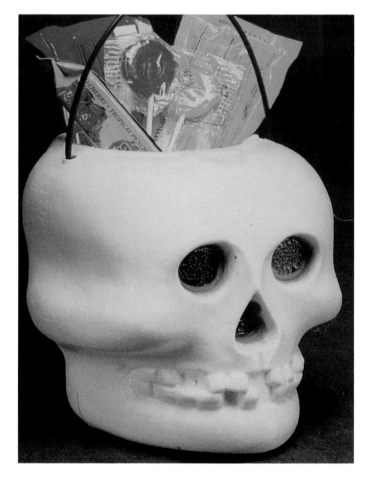

Blinky Brochure, #104 Skull container. (*Courtesy of Patty Gallagher Magnus.*)

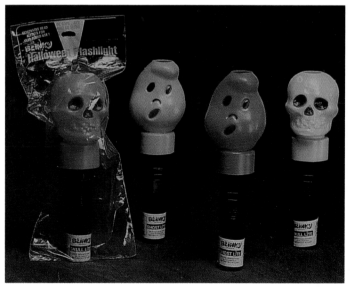

Blinky brochure, Neon colored flashlights. (Courtesy of *Patty Gallagher Magnus.*)

Blinky brochure, giant electric pumpkin window light. (*Courtesy of Patty Gallagher Magnus.*)

Blinky brochure, Electric party light sets. (*Courtesy of Patty Gallagher Magnus.*)

▲ 1103
14" ELECTRIC MR. BLINKY
Stickered • Pk. 12pc.

Blinky brochure, 14" electric Mr. Blinky. (*Courtesy of Patty Gallagher Magnus.*)

Vinyl flashlight, not marked, 8.5" x 3.25", orange and black vinyl, black paint. (*Courtesy of Mark and Judy Craven.*) $5-10.

Halloween barrette made in China, 1990s. (*Author's collection.*) $1-3.

Three new popular resin collectibles, two bears and a scarecrow,
1990s. (*Author's collection.*) $3-7 each.

Two new small vinyl witches.
Purple witch is by Willowbrook
Farms, made in China. Black witch
with cat marked "1991 BEE."
(*Author's collection.*) $3-5 each.

New cats, puffy black vinyl, made in Hong Kong. Left 3" x 2.25", right 3.25" x 1.38", (*Courtesy of Mark and Judy Craven.*) $3-5.

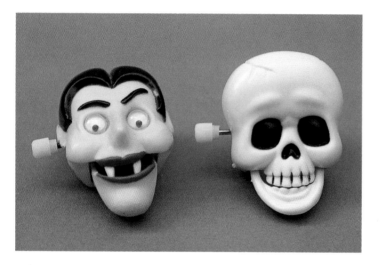

Witch puppet head, marked "285," 4.25" x 2.5", black soft vinyl, flesh-colored face with green eyes. (*Courtesy of Mark and Judy Craven.*) $5-10.

Candy sticks, all vinyl, E. Rosen Co. style, 1980s, each are 13" long, orange and black puffy vinyl. (*Courtesy of Dave and Ginny Wellington.*) $5-10.

Hallmark talking Dracula pin, 1987, Fun World talking skull pin, not dated, made in Hong Kong, Hallmark. (*Author's collection.*) $10-15. This type of pin will be very collectible soon, because of the excellent design.

Witch walker, Paper Magic Group, 1996, made in China, 2.75" x 1.75", black, green, and rust paint. She stands next to an Art Deco witch made of paper in 1934. (*Author's collection.*) $2-5. Note: Walkers have always been popular to collect.

Jack-o'-lantern pins, left one with a boo sign, made by Creative Creations, 1980s, 1.5" X 2", orange plastic, black and green paint, and string that moves the legs and arms. (*Courtesy of Mark and Judy Craven.*) $5-8.

Monster Pumpkin Box, Telstone Industries, 1980s, 6" square. (*Courtesy of Dave and Ginny Wellington.*)

Monster Pumpkin, Telstone Industries, 1980s, 6" x 5.5", orange plastic, battery operated, witch pops up out of jack-o'-lantern, eyes light up. (*Courtesy of Dave and Ginny Wellington.*) $25-35.

E. Rosen jack-o'-lantern, skeleton, and witch candy containers, made in Hong Kong, 4" x 1.75", clear, orange and white vinyl, black paint. Used for many years and still in use today. The tag used denotes age and the older tags are worth slightly more. (*Courtesy of Dave and Ginny Wellington.*) $3-5.

A new, boxed E. Rosen counter display, 1996. (*Author's collection.*)

Different labels on back of goblins. (*Author's collection.*)

Vinyl bat, marked made in China, 15" x 5". Black vinyl, brown paint with green eyes. (*Author's collection.*) $3-8.

Hallmark cat bucket with old papier-maché cat lantern. (*Author's collection.*) Hallmark cat bucket $10-15.

New vinyl candy stick tops made in China, right is from Hershey company, 1995, left is a Blinky top. 5" tall. (*Author's collection.*) $1-3.

Halloween Easter egg, not marked, 1960s, 2.5" x 1.75". Black and orange plastic egg that opens for candy. (*Courtesy of Mark and Judy Craven.*) $2-5.

Halloween pens, not marked, 5" long. (*Author's collection.*) $1-3 each.

Witch at Cauldron, marked "Hong Kong #555," 1960s, 5.5" x 3.5", orange plastic, green, black, and cream paint. (*Courtesy of Richard Miller.*) $10-15.

Blinking jack-o'-lantern, marked "Pat. Pend. Johannsen Taiwan." 1980s. 4.12" x 3.5". Orange plastic, plastic handle, clear plastic bulb. (*Courtesy of Mark and Judy Craven.*) $5-10.

Sparkler Gun, Creative Creations, 1976, made in Hong Kong, 4.38" x 3.38", orange plastic, black paint, metal trigger, eyes are cut out for sparks. (*Courtesy of Mark and Judy Craven.*) $15-25.

Jack-o'-lantern and cat flat cake top, not marked, 1980s, 3.25" x 5", orange plastic, black paint. (*Courtesy of Richard Miller.*) $5-8.

Jack-o'-lantern plastic candy container, packaged by Stichler Products, Reading, Pennsylvania, 1960s, new, 3" x 2.5", orange plastic, cutout features, covered with cellophane and tied with a ribbon. (*Author's collection.*) $3-5.

Haunted Halloween Express, New Bright Quality Toy, 1995, new in box. (*Courtesy of Mark and Judy Craven.*) $25-40.

Jack-o'-lantern plastic candy container packaged by Stichler Products, Reading, Pennsylvania, 19603, new, 8" x 4.25", orange plastic, black paint, original candy, witch party whistle. (*Courtesy of Richard Miller/Photo by Richard Miller.*) $8-12.

Jack-o'-lantern mold or cake decoration, made in China, 1990s, 5" x 3.5", all orange plastic. (*Courtesy of Mark and Judy Craven.*) $3-5.

McDonald's collectible, pop-out jack-o'-lantern, made in China, 1995, 3" tall, good quality new hard plastic. (*Author's collection.*) $2-5 each.

Jack-o'-lantern candy container, made in Hong Kong, 1990s, 3.25" x 4.75", orange and green plastic, black paint and black plastic handle, opens in middle. (*Courtesy of Mark and Judy Craven.*) $3-5.

Vinyl witch and bendy, witch is not marked, 1960s, 4.75" x 2.25",
semi-soft vinyl with black paint. Bendy made by Funworld, available
in catalog today. 3.25" x 5.25", orange, black, and green vinyl.
(*Courtesy of Mark and Judy Craven.*) Left $5-10, right $3-5.

Fun World Halloween clickers, made in Hong Kong, 1970s, 7.63" x
4.88", orange and black plastic, white paint (*Courtesy of Mark and
Judy Craven.*) $15-25.

Jack-o'-lantern vinyl squeek toy, not
marked, 1980s, 4.75" x 3.13", green and
orange vinyl (*Courtesy of Mark and Judy
Craven.*) $3-5.

Jack-o'-lantern with ribbon, not marked,
1980s, 8" x 4", orange vinyl with black
paint, black ribbon and handle. (*Courtesy of
Mark and Judy Craven.*) $5-8.

Inexpensive vinyl candy cup, thin vinyl
whistle, and two 1.25" water-filled pumpkins. A chenille pumpkin man from the
1940s hitches a ride in the cup. (*Author's
collection.*) $.50-2 each.

Fun World jack-o'-lantern wind-up toy,
made in China, 1.5" x 2", tongue goes in and
out as it rolls. (*Author's collection.*) $3-5.

Witch pencil sharpener, Manly Toy Limited, made in China, 4.5" x 1.5", on original card. (*Author's collection.*) $2-5.

Easter Unlimited, a Division of Fun World, modern Frankenstein and witch bendys. 4.5" x 4.25". (*Author's collection.*) $2-6 each.

Halloween spooky horns, made in China, 1990s, 7.25" x 3", orange and black plastic bottoms, orange and black soft vinyl tops, black, yellow, green, and white paint. (*Author's collection.*) $3-5 each.

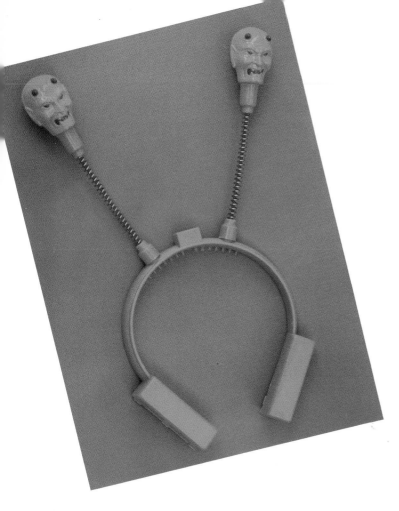

Halloween flashing antenna, made in China, 1990s, 10" x 8", orange plastic, green paint, springy antenna. (*Courtesy of Jordan Shock.*) $3-5.

Empire Industries new brochure, light-up pumpkin pail #7176, 1995, Page 5. (*Courtesy of Tom Prichard.*)

Jack-o'-lantern cup and place setting, made in China. (*Author's collection.*) $2-3.

Empire Industries new brochure, Halloween Bear #7462, 1995, Page 7. (*Courtesy of Tom Prichard.*)

Empire Industries new brochure, Autumn Wreath #7466, 1995, page 13. (*Courtesy of Tom Prichard.*)

Empire Industries new brochure, Scarecrow #7460, 1995, page 11. (*Courtesy of Tom Prichard.*)

Empire Industries, hard vinyl ghost with jack-o'-lantern and cat, 1990s, 3' tall. White vinyl with orange and black paint. (*Courtesy of Mark and Judy Craven.*) $15-25.

Empire Industries jack-o'-lantern with bangs, 1970, embossed Empire Plastic Corp. Made in U.S.A., 8" x 10", orange vinyl, black paint, black plastic handle. (*Author's collection.*) $10-15.

Empire Industries party pumpkins, 1979, Carolina Enterprises Inc., 11" x 6", orange vinyl, black paint. (*Author's collection.*) $7-10.

Pirate with mustache and patch, not marked, 1960s-'70s, 7" x 8", orange plastic, black paint, black plastic handle. (*Author's collection.*) $10-15.

100

Empire cat, right, marked "Carolina Enterprises Tarboro, North Carolina," 1990, 6" x 8.25", black vinyl, orange paint. Stands next to 1940s papier-maché cat lantern. (*Courtesy of Jordan Shock.*) $5-10.

Hershey kiss jack-o'-lantern, marked "1990 Hershey Foods Corp." 4.5" x 4.75", orange vinyl, paper stick on features. (*Courtesy of Kyrsten and Jeffrey Perhne.*) $5-10.

Empire light, jack-o'-lantern on corn shock, marked "Empire Plastic Corp.," 1969, made in U.S.A. 14.5" x 8", orange vinyl, black paint. (*Courtesy of Jordan Shock.*) $18-22.

Jack-o'-lantern with funny face and one tooth, no marks, 1970s, 7.5" x 10.5", orange vinyl, black paint, and black vinyl handle. (*Courtesy of Kyrsten and Jeffery Perhne.*) $10-15.

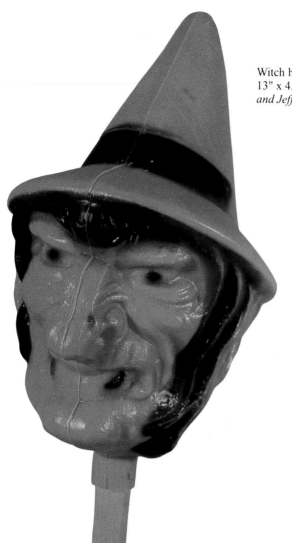

Witch head rattle, marked "Bayshore Ind. New York," 1960s-'70s, 13" x 4.5", orange vinyl, black paint, on stick. (*Courtesy of Kyrsten and Jeffrey Perhne.*) $15-20.

Jack-o'-lantern, orange vinyl, marked "Best Toy and Novelty," 1970s, 5" x 6". (*Author's collection.*) $3-5.

Two faced jack-o'-lantern, not marked, 1980s, 7" x 7", orange vinyl, black paint, fastens to light bulb, one face up/one face down for hanging or on lamp stand, (*Author's collection.*) $3-5.

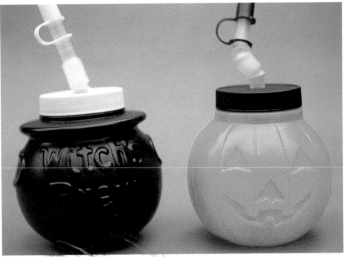

Jack-o'-lantern marked Liberty Plastic, Carolina California, 1980s, 6.6" x 6.5", orange vinyl, black paint, with black vinyl handle. (*Author's collection*.) $3-5.

Blinky's juice cups from Surf City, Huntington Beach, California. (*Author's collection.*) $1-2.

Jack-o'-lantern, not marked, Blinkys 1970s-'90s, 6" x 7", orange vinyl, black paint, black vinyl handle. (*Author's collection.*) $3-5.

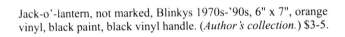

Scarry faced jack-o'-lantern with big eyes, not marked, 1970s, 7" x 7", orange thin vinyl, black and white paint. (*Author's collection.*) $15-20.

Jack-o'-lantern with mask and hair, not marked, 1970s, 8.5" x 9.5", orange vinyl, black paint. (*Author's collection.*) $15-20.

Jack-o'-lantern scarecrow man lamp, marked "Empire Plastic," 1969, made in U.S.A., 14.24" x 7", orange plastic, black paint. (*Courtesy of Mark and Judy Craven.*) $18-25.

Winking jack-o'-lantern, marked "Bayshore Ind. New York," 1970s, 9.5" x 9", orange vinyl, black paint, black vinyl handle. (*Courtesy of Mark and Judy Craven.*) $10-15.

Jack-o'-lantern on top of cat lamp, not marked, 1980s, 13.5" x 7.75", orange vinyl, black paint. (*Courtesy of Mark and Judy Craven.*) $5-10.

Witch and jack-o'-lantern lamp, marked "General Foam Castings Corp. Norfolk, Va.," 1990s, 14.5" x 6.75", orange vinyl, black paint. (*Courtesy of Mark and Judy Craven.*) $10-15.

1993 Trendmasters indoor jack-o'-lantern light, foam with a hard plastic bottom, very realistic looking, 9.5" x 9". (*Author's collection.*) $5-8.

Owl on a jack-o'-lantern lamp, not marked, beautiful design, 1990s, 13" x 9", orange vinyl, black paint. (*Courtesy of Mark and Judy Craven.*) $20-25.

Jack-o'-lantern with a pointed hat lamp, not marked, 1980s, 12.5" x 7.38", orange vinyl, black paint. (*Courtesy of Mark and Judy Craven.*) $5-12.

Witch with cauldron lamp, not marked, Bayshore Ind. 1970s-'80s, 14.5" x 6", orange and black vinyl, black paint. (*Courtesy of Mark and Judy Craven.*) $18-25.

Vinyl two-sided jack-o'-lantern, unmarked, 9" x 7", orange vinyl with black paint, $10-15. (*Courtesy of Richard Miller/Photo by Richard Miller.*)

Other side of two-faced jack-o'-lantern.

Jack-o'-lantern on cat lamp, not marked, Empire Ind., made in the U.S.A., 1960s, 13.5" x 7.75", orange vinyl, black paint. (*Courtesy of Thomas M. Weber and Terry M. Weber.*) $15-20.

Jack-o'-lantern lamp with derby hat, embossed "Bayshore Ind. Inc.," 1960s-'70s, 11" x 5.5", orange vinyl, black paint. (*Courtesy of Mark and Judy Craven.*) $10-18.

Empire gift set for baby's first Halloween. Set includes a bib, bottle, and Halloween keys. (*Author's collection.*) $5-8.

Union Products brochure, witch with pumpkin, #55520, 20.5" high. (*Courtesy of Don Featherstone.*)

Lamps, 1990, orange vinyl, black paint: left, Union Products Tweat #5260, 14.5" x 7"; right, Twik #5258, 1990," 13" x 5". (*Author's Collection*) $30-40 set.

Union Products brochure, witch candle, #55740, 36" high. (*Courtesy of Don Featherstone.*)

Union Products brochure, Halloween scene on moon, #56160, 19" diameter. (*Courtesy of Don Featherstone.*)

Union Products brochure, jack-o'-lantern on moon, #56200, 19" diameter. (*Courtesy of Don Featherstone.*)

Union Products brochure, owl scene on moon, #56140, 19" diameter. (*Courtesy of Don Featherstone.*)

Union Products brochure, witch on moon, #56180, 19" diameter. (*Courtesy of Don Featherstone.*)

Union Products brochure, Mr. Crow, #56220, 14" tall. (*Courtesy of Don Featherstone.*)

Union Products brochure, Vulture, #56060, 14" tall. (*Courtesy of Don Featherstone.*)

Union Products brochure, Haunted House, #55720, 24" high. (*Courtesy of Don Featherstone.*)

Union Products brochure, Pumpkin Trio #55760, 30" long. (*Courtesy of Don Featherstone.*)

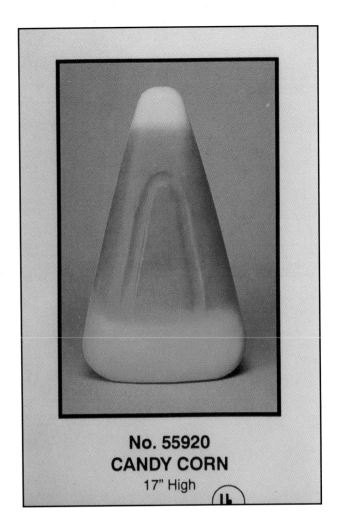

No. 55920
CANDY CORN
17" High

Union Products brochure, Goblin with sign #55820, 30" high. (*Courtesy of Don Featherstone.*)

Union Products brochure, Candy Corn #55920, 17" high. (*Courtesy of Don Featherstone.*)

No. 55460
HALLOWEEN CAT
17 1/2" High

Listed

Union Products brochure, Halloween cat #55460, 17.5" high. (*Courtesy of Don Featherstone.*)

New collectible arts-and-crafts cloth Halloween dolls with vinyl pirate jack-o'-lantern. Some are Hallmark and others are Russ and various other companies. (*Author's collection.*) $15-25 each.

Union Products ghost coming out of a pumpkin, #5254, orange and white vinyl, black paint, designed by, and embossed with signature of, Don Featherstone, 1992. 21" x 9.5" (*Author's collection.*) $18-25.

Union Products Witch #5252, 1992, 20.5" high, orange vinyl, black paint. Designed by, and embossed with signature of, Don Featherstone. (*Courtesy of Mark and Judy Craven.*) $35-50.

Bibliography

Cohen, Hennig and Tristian Potter Coffin. *America Celebrates*. Detroit, Michigan: Visible Ink Press, 1991.

Gordon, Ellen. *Hallmark: The Collection Connection*. Laguna Hills, California: Ellen Gordon, 1996-97.

Hanlon, Bill. *Plastic Toys: Dimestore Dreams of the 40s & 50s*. Atglen, Pennsylvania: Schiffer Publishing, 1993.

Hunt, Tamara and Renfo, Nancy. *Celebrate*. Austin, Texas: Nancy Renfo Studios, 1987.

Ickis, Marguerite. *The Book of Festival Holidays*. New York, New York: Dodd Mead and Company, 1964.

Resource: The National Plastic Center and Museum, Leominster, Massachusetts.